Front Lines

Voices from the Toronto Writers Collective

TORONTO WRITERS COLLECTIVE

Toronto Writers Collective Press

Front Lines: Voices From The Toronto Writers Collective

Published by Toronto Writers Collective Press
Editors: Jesse Cohoon, Richard Mozer, Puneet Dutt, Jay Teitel, Susan Ksiezopolski, Bänoo Zan, Susan Turk Mozer
Front Cover Art: Naomi Hendrickje Laufer / Black Rose
For reprints, permissions and more information please contact
info@torontowriterscollective.ca

ISBN 978-1-7750247-0-5

Printed in Canada

Front Lines and the Write On! Workshops were developed with the assistance of:

THE Kaszas GROUP

BMO Wealth Management
BMO Nesbitt Burns

and artsVest™ Toronto is operated by Business for the Arts with the support of the Toronto Arts Council and the Government of Canada

Bft Business for the Arts / Les affaires pour les arts

TORONTO ARTS COUNCIL | FUNDED BY THE CITY OF TORONTO

Funded by the Government of Canada | Financé par le gouvernement du Canada | Canada

With the support of:
The Toronto Public Library and the librarians and staff at:
Evelyn Gregory Branch, Parkdale Branch, St. Jamestown Branch, Queen Saulter Branch, Ralph Thornton Centre

1 2 3 4 5 6 7 8 9 10

Book Cover Design:

Naomi Hendrickje Laufer, also known as Black Rose, was born in Toronto and studied various disciplines focusing on the arts as a means of communication and expression. She concentrates mainly in three art forms, dance, poetry and visual arts, including wearable art for good causes. Naomi strives to incorporate healing through the arts and to give voice to those neglected in society. She comes from a family of artists and has travelled through Europe with them. She has worked in Switzerland as an au pair and studied printmaking in the south of France. Naomi tries to see the 'melody' carried by individual members of humanity in the hope of learning from one another's differences and evolving through a revolution of empathy.

"I tried to, capture the essence of transformation in the cover illustration by portraying Daphne turning into a tree to escape Apollo's advances and hence reflecting the words of the writers within the anthology who had transformed their thoughts, feelings and ideas into a literary style unique to each individual."

Down the deepest darkest well I fell
And in the bottom I found broken stars that drowned
And now bathed in stardust I awaken to find
Myself on a scarlet hill frozen
I closed my eyes and a one-winged dove flew over me
I grasped her delicate wing and floated with her
And slept with her on the horizon where there was breath
Like a cherub without an eye I could see the dawn as through
a telescope
and the gates closed.

Introduction

It is my privilege to introduce our first published anthology, **Front Lines: Voices From The Toronto Writers Collective**. This book is testament to the creative genius we all have within when given opportunity to explore our authentic voice. Many of our writers never had the chance to cultivate and share their work, to see the impact of their words and the connections they create in our shared community. Writing is an act both simple and profound. Simple, for we all are writers, as poet and writing teacher Pat Schneider says, "If you can talk, you can write, for talking is like writing on air." Writing is both simple and profound. Simple, for we are all writers. Profound, for writing changes lives. This first anthology illustrates that; our writers illuminate the full vibrant color of their creativity.

These are stories that pull down the walls and bring us back to the living heart of our city. These are stories of bravery in the living of difficult day to day, stories of coming of age, poetry of redemption and rhythm. These are stories that go deep into the reality of experiences often shared for the first time. In short, these are stories of insight from those rarely heard and they will knock your socks off.

The TWC is proud to publish the original work of our Write On! writers, who worked diligently with our committed mentors over several months. This publication is a true milestone in the growth of our writers and our organization. TWC began its first creative writing workshop at the Friendship Center Homeless Drop In Shelter on Dundas Street in 2012, with one workshop and two writers that we dragged in. We reiterated that we wanted to hear the stories ONLY THEY could tell. And could they tell stories! From that small beginning the Toronto Writers Collective now runs over a dozen sustained writing workshops in the city's most marginalized neighbourhoods, encouraging voice and changing lives through the power of expression. Our writers enrich us with discovered truths that surprise, enlighten and emancipate.

I thank the writers, the mentors (Puneet Dutt, Bänoo Zan, Jay Teitel and Susan Ksiezopolski) of our WRITE ON! initiative, and all the volunteers and supporters of the work that we do. I also wish to thank Naomi Hendrickje Laufer/Black Rose for the beautiful original artwork created for our cover, and a special thank you to Jesse Cohoon, our Program Manager for his tireless work and dedication to the Write On! project and the creation of this anthology.

These voices strengthen and enrich our city, celebrate the diversity of experience and emphasize our shared humanity. To our writers, Congratulations! To our readers, Enjoy!

With Gratitude,

Susan Turk Mozer

Founder

Toronto Writers Collective

Message from the Mentors

From all of us to each of you, our featured writers — congratulations! By adding your voice and your talent through your writing, you've made an invaluable contribution to this eclectic and fascinating representation of the work produced by the Toronto Writers Collective. Your participation and commitment to the Write On! workshops have paid off. Your words, woven into your storytelling, prose and poetry, have created a truly impressive and profound collection.

The richness in these pages speaks to the diversity of your human experience, and is inspirational because it speaks to ours as well. It has been an honour and a privilege to share this journey with each of you. Don't forget to send us an invite to your future launches and award parties as you continue to grow your craft and share your writing with the world.

Keep writing and telling your stories; the world needs to hear them all!

Puneet Dutt   Susan Ksiezopolski   Jay Teitel   Bänoo Zan

Table of Contents

Table of Contents

The Day of the Air Show

p. a. eng

You fell down the stairs last Sunday and hurt your knee and shoulder. It would help if you had some sleep. You don't know what you drank but you awoke on the wood stairs in some different apartment building around the corner. Some good Samaritan had covered you with a light blanket that smelled freshly laundered. You folded it before you left and placed it on the banister. Compared to your place, the stairway was well swept, and there was a welcome mat at each door. For the last couple of months you have had a blackout once a week. Safety is a lost wheel. A two-headed dog with a monstrous roar awaits you. With luck something might calm you down like a familiar face, the spotting of a fancy car, some interesting snatch of talk on the street, the liquor store opens in five minutes. Thank God you still have money in the bank.

The boisterous working activity of Chinatown enacts around you in brute confusion. Behind you a man pushes a line of steel shopping wagons. The metal jangling makes you wince. Jesus is the first word that springs out of your mouth. Then, the most awfully vulgar swear word followed by the next word, Christ. The once still flame in your mind flickers on the verge of paranoia. The blue sky is weeping on you. You are a walking scrap heap two days awake on August 9th, a Saturday morning in Toronto. A year ago, on this day, you were deported back to Canada from Athens, Greece. It's an anniversary and you hope to find Marica smiling at her address at the women's shelter.

The alley behind the liquor store has a good clean niche to sit down with your cold Australian beer imported in a large maximum sized can with a small circle of white stars in reference to their flag. The summer wind is a gentle surprise as you sit on the ground with your back against the wall and your forearms resting easy on your bent knees. A middle-aged Chinese woman in a brown uniform nervously squints over her glasses as she walks by pulling a small cart of vegetables. She ignores you as you raise the heavy can to your lips. The smoky taste of the Australian beer greets your tongue delectably. From a short distance away, on your right-hand side, a truck is hydraulically unloading food behind a popular Asian eatery. Spouts of sound break, pause, pass and snort. A seagull is aloft and gliding overhead. You can hear the loud quick screech and regard it as a good omen.

Marica is probably somewhere in the middle of a conversation with herself blowing cannabis in the air, unfolding her artless hype, alone on a stage of mystery. She made you laugh when she pulled out the front neckline of her white Parasuco T-shirt with her two hands and bent her face into the open gap and yelled, "GET OUT OF THERE NOW." You can hold hands with her youthful charisma. She is never sleazy. Her white blondness crashes the gates of your sanity. You know you shouldn't be with her. Marica is a reckless wonder. She never despairs. You asked her if she had any bad habits and she said deadpan, "I litter." She also told you that she was a former addict and stripper.

"I first got introduced to hash while I was stripping. I was 18. I left a foster home and came to the big city, got this stripper job and learned how to climb a pole naked, so we started smoking hash and a few months later some girls brought some coke to work. I got addicted and everything went downhill. I lost my car, my fur coat and then I got fired for coming in late all the time. I went from one club to another and I couldn't straighten out. I was a full-blown crackhead."

Suddenly, the plain blue sky is creased and swiped over by a conquering funnel of roars as a squadron of fighter jets scream across the vanity of space. The Air Show has started at the waterfront. It would take at least an hour to walk south-west to the grandstand. You get up and try to walk straight but that is never certain after guzzling two large cans of beer on an empty stomach. Hunger is a lost percussion.

You decide to rest at a small park where a couple of long-haired guys wearing Blue Jays baseball hats are throwing a frisbee. You walk to a shaded corner with a row of three wood benches. At the end of the row, a young woman is opening a large flat box of pizza. Her girlfriend is lifting a slice out of the box.

"They are good, they always give you double cheese with the special slice,"

"Never order the anchovies,"

"How can anyone put that in their mouth? You'd have to be brain dead,"

"And who needs that?"

They high five'd their hands with a resounding clap.

You lie down at the other end of the row of benches as another avalanche of searing white noise cuts open the sky. The pizza smell invades your consciousness. Voices of the frisbcc players scatter back and forth.

"Nice grab dude."

"I'm in the groove now, okay, long toss, take it!"

The pitiable wail of a fire truck adds another familiar text in the summer air. The wood slats of the bench feel made for your back while your head lies crunching against two other cans of beer inside your shoulder bag. The dizzy migration to this small park has finally ended as your eyes close.

Before you can fall asleep a woman's voice urgently snaps.

"Are you alright? Angie, Angie!!"

You sit up slowly and see one woman clapping her hand vigorously on the other woman's back. The woman with her mouth open is choking. Her arms are stiff at her side. Her hands are clenched in fists. The girlfriend bangs her hand at the upper back region hoping to dislodge the block and she cries out.

"Help! Someone help us!!"

The young choking woman has fallen panicking on the grass. Something registers in your mind, a commercial on TV and you stand up and rush over to help. The frisbee players have hurried over. The young woman lying on the grass is choking madly. Her young face is in fearful agony and has turned a green and dark colour. She is lying sideways and frantically kicking her heels into the grass, spinning herself in circles.

You order the guys to pick her up and you walk around behind her and grip her around her waist and forcefully give a yank into her stomach and the chunk of food pops out of her mouth and she instantly sucks in air and is relieved.

You feel stunned as you step back and retrieve your shoulder bag. The relieved young woman has one hand on her chest and is sitting down on the bench and taking deep breaths of air. The frisbee players stand next to her and offer kind words. One of them is holding a can of pop for her. Her girlfriend thanks you and you are nodding and walking away. Something has pawned your reality. You had acted so calmly as if you knew what had to be done and what would happen.

You walk back into the sunny swirl of Chinatown and feel astonished at what occurred at the park. You saved someone's life. Your senses have perked. You are awake but you feel dazed. You remember the commercial. It was a couple of years ago. It was a public announcement about a choking victim and how to save the person. You lean your shoulder against the outside wall of a Chinese grocery store as shoppers pass by in the glowing sun. The decision of that isolated instant prevented an atrocity. The young woman was resurrected. If you had not been there... Your eyes blankly search the ground. Your face remains impassive as the flexing motion of the packed street eludes you. You shake your head slowly and try in vain to summarize the events of the past two days. Unnoticing the heckling merchant voices of the Asiatic street you zip open your bag and pull out a king-sized can of beer. If you had been more drunk you would have not reached the park. After a quick gulp you put the can of beer on the ground. You close your eyes and send a prayer of thanks for your life. You walk to the next block and as usual there is a panhandler sitting on the corner. You take out your last can of beer from your shoulder bag and hand it to the scruffy guy and he smiles and responds to you in a gravelly voice.

"Thanks bro, and good luck."

It's noon and time to go home and sleep. A gorgeous summer wind gusts from behind as you amble up Spadina Avenue.

Nothing Fits

Roberta Taylor

I am too poor to pay attention
I have no new clothes
nothing fits in my closet
nothing fits in my thoughts

I don't get to say what's on
my mind

I can't remember everything
I do day to day
nothing fits in my heart
nothing fits in my soul

My loneliness is not yours
My illness is not either,
You can't cure me by
Passing me by
but you don't notice if
if I live or die

Nothing fits in my soul
Nothing fits, I'm too old

My Art and thoughts
are my friends
Poets are the ones
Who watch and wait
but often Poets are just
Too late

To change your mind
Do you have change for me?
I don't want it for much
I just am poor
so nothing fits of
    my clothes
Some are too big
    others too old

Nothing Fits in
        my imagination
I stand on the Fault
Line between being old
and not noticed
no one sees me on
the streetcar
unless I cry or piss myself

Then I'm embarrassed
because nothing Fits
to change into

nothing Fits
        I Feel sad
nothing Fits
        but
Still I'm glad
I'm free enough
not to judge
    anyone but
        me.

Where Are You From, Really?

Rana Khan

I am from Varanasi, India
A country ancient and wise, but lately cursed
With warring godheads, amidst a fractured people and their histories.
I'm also from Aligarh, India
Where ideas romanced and seduced me, and it was here,
Beside the red brick walls covered with yellow roses, that love finally claimed me.
I'm also from Jeddah, Saudi Arabia,
Where ideas are miscarried or stillborn, and mourned quietly.
The landscape of black-clad women and white-clad men gives no succour.
My two babies, born here, carry a stigma forever in their passports.
Who knew then of a certain date in September?
I'm also from Dubai, United Arab Emirates
Ah that city of magic and dreams, built by the unsung who toiled in the merciless sun,
The city corrupted by money and many, now its charms seem tired even to itself.
Lately, I'm from Toronto, Canada
Joining thousands of others in search of new destinies,
Nameless, faceless, yet identified by the struggle to make this country our own.
Yes, I'm from all this and more,
I'm also of parents who died too early, and sisterly love that still sings across the oceans.
But a question now for you: where I'm from, does it matter,
When it's where I'm going that preoccupies me most days?

The Guy

Colin Buchanan

I'm the guy sitting on the park bench reading a newspaper who can't tell you anything he's just read. I'm the guy standing at the edge of the water thinking of dry land. I'm the guy at the end of the bar wearing shades with his hat pulled over his eyes. I'm the guy lying in bed trying to get you to talk so I may not have to. I'm the guy who could ruin your life. I'm the guy who could save your life. I'm the guy who cuts himself with the knife your boyfriend gave me. I'm the guy who isn't even going to try to make you cry, but I'm the guy who knows what to say when you do. I'm the guy who misses you so much it hurts almost as much as when we're together. I'm the guy with the answers so long as the question is framed to my liking. I'm the guy patiently waiting for you to tell me what guy you want me to be. That guy.

Abandonment

Jose Mario Moreira de Oliveira

I'm walking down a cold and dark street feeling dizzy. Don't remember how I got here. My mind feels disconnected from my body, like an immaterial passenger sitting on the back of my eyes. My legs autonomously take me somewhere. Tears pour from my eyes, but I do not feel pain or anger, just mute sadness.

Right across the street, I see her. She doesn't look like herself, but somehow I know it's her. The street is full of cars speeding as if on a highway, still I have to cross and be with her. My legs automatically work by themselves, strangely taking me through the car's dangerous gaps with enough precision to leave death just a few millimeters behind.

As I finally reach the other side, I fall. My legs tired of their independence, of doing all the work themselves. With a strange instinct, a strong moment of desire, I cling to her waist. I smell her. I feel that inexplicable feeling I have every time I hold her. She looks at me with her big beautiful, shiny, apathetic eyes. Eyes that have looked inside mine crying promised eternal love. Eyes that are now empty. Even though I hold her with all my strength, she easily disengages from my grasp. My arms feel as feeble as tissue paper. Helpless, and kneeling on the ground, I see with desperate eyes how beautiful she is.

My vision does not last long. In moments, her sharp kick in the chin makes me lose consciousness. On the ground, free from the paranoia of the real world, I dream. We're making love. I sniff her hair and touch her perfect face contorted with pleasure, my hands feast on her perfect breasts. In that moment, we are the size of the universe. Nothing else exists, only that moment, only that spasm running through our bodies flooding us with happiness and hope.

In that moment as short as that orgasmic dream, I see our children and I see her, now an old woman. I feel her wrinkled hand in mine. In that infinitesimal second before falling into that dark abyss I wish only to never wake up and see the cruel light of reality again.

Women – Hand In Hand

Penelope Klees

Women STAND
Hand in Hand
Faith to Faith
No colour-coded
HERE
In this, my LAND

Be you Black, White
Indigenous, Asian
or Multi-Heritage
I CARE NOT
if you be
Christian, Muslim
Hindu or Jew
or of no particular religious hue

We've suffered
YES,
I'll join you
Hand in Hand with You

As Women – We STAND
Our Oprahs
Harriet Tubmans
Amy Goodmans

Modern Women
Young Women of Bahrain
PUT IN JAIL

for saying
I have a Right
TO BE HEARD!!!

ME LADY – MS. PATEL
OF PAKISTAN
Fought alone
after acid
thrown in FACE

Born into poverty
In Pakistan
After a great injustice
Done to her
By her patriarchal husband
Seven years he got -
She WON!!!

Courageous Me Lady of Pakistan
My TRUE Heroine

Women
Our Ancestors-Warriors
Nzenghor, Ashantawaa

Chinese Women
Bound of Foot
Feet Bound,
Pressed tight
With cotton cloth
Ever more smaller
in cloth of cotton

And made to wear
Cotton cloth – wooden shoes
Unable to walk or stand
for long

Ancestors/ Modern Women
I SALUTE YOU
I stand
Hand in Hand
With YOU.

Who Am I

Dee Hope

Who am I, the music of my heart speaks to you
I will tell you more
I am the rhythm that speaks to your mind
The bass in your face, funk replaced
I am the quiver, timed symphonically to your size
You thought you would deny

I am the picture, painted with timeless renaissance
Like the reggae beat in your eardrums jamming
the truth of blues
Emancipate yourself in rhythmic syncopation,
free your mind
Tune into my prime, real estate of soul
I am the song of your fears, felt inside
The words captured, tears released the pride
The love that would not die, why?

Don't just go through the motion when I rock you
from side to side
Put a pep in your step, aligned and timed
Feel the rhythm of my size
The drumbeat of my existence
Throbbing your inner core
Now realizing that you are wanting more
The music, the story, the song, the permeated truth

Who am I, I am the rhythm in your soul
Now alert to the pain you caused
Acoustically forlorn, who am I

I am the song that lives on, let it be
No woman no cry, I am the music born in your thighs
That penetrates your body, soul and mind
I am the music, the pride of yesteryear
Still current, often remembered
Ain't no mountain high enough for me
Just standing there, music around me
I am the music, songs of freedom proclaimed
Who am I, I am the song in my music, the rhythm
sustained
I am the woman who loves music and life
He never loved me, the music is alive in me, I am music

Better Late Than Never

Ward Smyth

1

Seems so long ago
You were taken away.
What I wouldn't give
For one more day.
A million things to tell you
That won't make it better.
But it's true what they say,
Better late than never.

2

It was you n' you alone
Who helped me appreciate music,
But in my twenties with drugs a plenty
That's when I thought I'd lose it.
Luckily a decade later
An artist gave a spark n' lit my fire,
I know you're near me, at least in theory
So that helps me reach even higher.
Cuz of you, it's my desire
My one love, my true fate,
If you were here right now
I know you'd say it's never too late.
N' it was you n' Uncle Ross,
Who also taught me compassion.
Insisted I maintain my brain
When that shit wasn't in fashion.
Used to get mad at you n' dad
For keepin' me off teams n' kids to play with,

Thinkin' I'd get lumped less
If I learned how to play Beethoven's Fifth.
Hated playin' piano for hours,
While my friends played, I's at a recital.
A kid, not knowin' what I did
Cuz that stuff right now is fuckin' vital.
I wanted to be a fuckin' child,
I resented you both for many years,
Now that resentment is buried in sediment,
It rusted my gears with many tears.
But I'm so damn sorry mom,
For the amazin' gift you gave to me.
Sometimes somethin' so close to you
That it's the last thing you can see.

3

I remember when dad was gone,
You had to come down on me.
You tried to intimidate, I just faked,
You were too sweet n' stood 5'3.
You didn't wanna be the bad one
But for whatever reason, you had to.
I bet that you were more scared than I was
N' after, I know you felt bad too.
Cuz I know that kinda treatment
It just wasn't in your nature,
'Cept that one time I's in Grade 5
N' my gym teacher unknowingly made ya.
I's playin' soccer on lunch time
Slipped, fell n' broke my leg,
Got carried to the school like a fool,
He thought it was a bruise despite my beg.

Teacher then pulled up a chair
N' straightened my leg up on it.
That's the one time you scared me
If I can be perfectly honest.
I heard you tearin' a new one, mum
From behind the closed door,
After a while I cracked a smile
N' all I could think of was "give him more."
That day you were my savior,
Yeah, you did what any other would,
But regardless, you still covered me
With the love that only a mother could.
I never got to say thank you,
For that among other things,
Every time you pushed the world n' curled
Me up under your lovin' wings.

4

Subconsciously I tell you, Mom,
That I ain't comin' home,
N' how shocked n' blown away I am
That I made it on my own, alone.
Wanna pick up the phone
But that's just too long distance,
No company dials off wishes,
And all I'd get is a dial tone.
Mom, your baby's grown,
I know you're lookin' down on me,
N' I hope you don't frown on me
For my poor decisions, I know they're plenty.
I know what you meant
When you came down on me

For mockin' that song, you see,
Cuz it is me against the world, times three.
I hit these dark places,
Where I all I see are snarked faces,
Makin' me jitter n' more bitter
Than a man with Deuces when the world has Aces.
Like I'm claustrophobic
N' given cramped spaces.
But I work within my means,
It's in my genes, so I thank the gracious.
I know this world's spacious
N' I could have it worse,
But I'd still put it in a verse
N' rehearse till it's in reverse or I'm in a hearse.
Don't hate me for how I curse,
It's a part of who I am,
N' despite some content you know I'm right
When I say you'd be my biggest fan.

Musical Deafness

Tracey de Boer

He tells me hip-hop isn't music.

He tells me this while he's cooking us dinner, pasta aglio e olio, an Italian recipe from his grandmother. I admire the way he moves around the kitchen: fluid, practiced, the way I imagine a real adult man would.

We're in his apartment — a large West Coast one bedroom with nothing on the walls. He's been living here a couple of years now, but told me he'd never decorated because he didn't want it to feel like "home." Or was it that he didn't want to have to take anything off when he moved? I can't remember. Either way, there's something about blank walls that's unsettling. There's a feeling of incompleteness — a yearning.

He puts on his music — power metal. He tells me that this is music; the proper form of music. No lyrics. As I listen, I think about a man I've heard about recently who was diagnosed with "musical deafness." To him, all music sounds like pots and pans clanging together. I feel sad for this man and wonder, what must it be like to never hear what everyone else hears?

He goes back to cooking and I step out to the balcony. It's too hot in there; between the cooking and musical noise and that sick feeling I get from not speaking up. The air is cool and inviting. Although I can't see the ocean from here, the wind is carrying that oceany smell — clean, soft and salty. I imagine this is what air is always supposed to be like. The further from the ocean it gets, the more polluted it becomes; it takes on the scent of wherever it is, the city, the noise, grit, dirt, smog and soot.

He often spoke of his family's origins. How his parents

met; his desire to make his Catholic parents proud. My favourite was about his grandmother — his Nonnina. How she was sharp around the edges and kept a gun in the house to shoot city animals who would wander into her yard. Instead of calling for help, she'd shoot and bury them herself. One time, she'd cornered a skunk who'd wandered, unluckily, into her backyard. As the two faced off, the skunk sprayed her out of self-defence. But without missing a beat, she peeled off her cotton house dress with one hand and took aim with the other.

When he told me this one, I laughed. It was absurd. Normally I would've been disturbed to hear of an old Italian woman killing animals in her backyard, but the image is so surreal I can hardly fault her for living out her old-world ways. His parents eventually took her gun away and I almost felt sad for her. I guess I saw her as the one person in his stories who was making room for herself where she was.

His stories became a highlight of our time together. But in that time I came to develop a theory about good storytellers. While they talk well, they don't listen with nearly the same level of ease.

We're walking back to my apartment after a movie. The air has that soft salty perfume of ocean, more present after the sun goes down. In response to the movie, I find myself talking about what (or who) I think God is: some underlying thing that unites us. Something we dissolve into and become a part of once we die. Before I can say I think it's a beautiful idea, he cuts me off—

"No," he says. "That's wrong."

As if there's some certain fact of the matter I am wrong about (maybe there is?). As if there was some textbook we'd both studied and I'd misunderstood (maybe there was?). Anyway, he begins to talk over me and tells me how God is not an impersonal God. He tells me God is a personal God. He tells me if we were all a part of God — in my sense of the word — then we cannot have a relationship with God. And relationship is everything. So I'm wrong.

I didn't realize that what I was describing was "impersonal." The interaction leaves a thorn in my chest and we walk the rest of the way to my apartment in silence.

As we brush our teeth in my tiny bathroom, I look at him in the reflection of the bathroom mirror.

"You kind of talked over me," I say, which is an understatement.

Why do I qualify myself when what I meant to say was: "That was rude."

Or: "I didn't deserve that."

Or: "Please don't treat me that way."

Maybe this ability to speak up for oneself comes with age. My attempts so often seem to fall flat and I'm left with this haze that I can't quite name. We hug and sort of make up and he falls asleep, but I stay awake, listening to the wind rattle my bedroom windows, thinking of the ocean whipping against the rocks.

As we each became more and more like ourselves in the relationship, I began to feel smaller. On multiple occasions I grasped clumsily for thc words to describe what I felt was happening to me. "If we were two shapes, your shape would be overlapping mine," I think I said at one point.

I've lost count of the times he became angry; he'd call me up to start a fight. It would start off normal enough, "How're you?" "Fine." "How was your day?" "Fine." Then things would shift.

He'd bring up something I'd said weeks, maybe months, ago. He'd raise his voice; he'd explain things to me in excruciating detail why what I believed couldn't possibly be right, and what did I mean when I said that? I never had strong responses either, only "I disagree," but nothing else.

There was something I forgot to mention about the walls in his apartment. I guess they weren't completely blank. A hole had been punched into one of them, between the bedroom and bathroom. I should've recognized the look of it. There used to be holes like that in my house too — the morning after I'd hear my parents fight. Drywall with cracks spread outward. But things like that seemed normal. "Oh, he's just passionate." "It was an accident." "It's okay, you can patch it up, it's only drywall."

Around this time, I got a job at a resource center for people with AIDs and HIV. It was a community-run space and I enjoyed the work and the people and spent my time bundling clean syringes or restocking the free condoms and pamphlets.

I quickly made a friend there — a middle-aged mother who'd run away from her abusive partner to protect her child. She'd been a fugitive for over 15 years, moving around with her daughter. She was tall with long silver hair and a big personality. She swore a lot and always called me "my dear."

"I'm the one who's been in all the papers," she told me the first day I'd met her. This startled me but I soon found how easy she was to be around. She was wise and angry — two things I don't often see in one person.

I often asked him to come visit me at work.

"Meet me for lunch?" "Pick me up after my shift?" "Come meet who I work with?" But he didn't want to. He made it about morality — he didn't agree that they "supported drug use" as he put it.

"But it's not just about that," I'd say. He'd never admit it, but I thought that maybe he was just afraid.

One afternoon we walked along the shore; the waves were persistent, the sound both consuming and calming. I looked around for a good piece of driftwood to sit on. The shore was always changing. Even if I found a comfortable log to perch on and watch the waves, it would be gone the next day — reclaimed by the water and pulled back deep into the ocean. At first I found this disorienting — I had a hard time finding my way around when landmarks were changing overnight. But after a while I came to find it eerie and enchanting.

I watched him search for smooth rocks to toss into the water. His hands were cracked and dry, almost painful looking. I wondered how long they'd been like that. He picked up a few stones and handed me a couple before throwing his into the water and continuing on.

I'd begun to understand the way he saw the world. He categorized information into Catholic or Not-Catholic. Things that fit his way of understanding were sorted neatly into the Catholic folder. The rest — everything that didn't fit, or was messy or complicated or wrong, didn't deserve to be sorted through. The rest was put into the Not-Catholic folder — a dark place to be bolted shut. I think for a little while I must've fit into one of those categories. He would tell me which of my behaviors seemed Catholic, or what movies had a Catholic or Not-Catholic message. Maybe it was his way of making the world feel more manageable; like the stories he told and the arguments he tried to win.

I looked at the handful of rocks he'd given me; between the smooth skipping stones there was a small piece of animal bone. I wondered if he knew what he'd handed me. I looked up to say something but he was already too far to hear me over the sound of the waves.

What Age?

Penelope Klees

HOW OLD ARE YOU?!!
WHAT AGE ARE YOU??
REPLY
"WISDOM IS MY AGE!!!"
YOUNG
SOMETIMES TOO!!
WISDOM IS/CAN BE THEIR AGE TOO!!

TAKEN FOR GRANTED??
Many withdrew
Couldn't stand the judgement.
Society played out to you??

SHRINKING FROM SOCIETY.
DON'T LOOK RIGHT??
THEIR VIEW!!!

DON'T WORRY!!!
Young, Elder, Middle-aged
(Homeless) TOO
NEXT TIME THEY ASK
HOW OLD ARE YOU??
REPLY!!!
"WISDOM IS MY AGE"
FINISH IT THERE TOO!!

The Addict Within

Stacey Bowen

Back then, in the very beginning of going cold turkey, she had only three weeks clean under her belt, since her last daily consumption of assorted colorful pills that would take her to her greatest highs, running mentally away her nightmares of terrible woes. Trying to stay clean and sober from seconds to moments was at best extremely difficult for her. She missed the sense of power and control she felt when selecting her self-treatment from each pill. She missed the amusement of pondering questions out to the universe of her small apartment, she'd ask herself "Which colored pill to consume next?" She needed them to cover her moments of self-disgust. She always looked forward to using first thing in the mornings, then once she got to her pivotal high, she would vacate into her tiny shrunken world because her thoughts got too real to imagine her life or anyone going through the emotional upheaval that she did.

Her wake-up morning pills gave her the chance to change the way she was feeling before she could see or hear the world. It put such a strain on her to think clearly. Her sense of power came from conjuring up her own sense of reality. She lived the hours by night and day getting rid of any feelings that were uncomfortable because she didn't know how to handle the memories of the vacant blank stares, the wet foamy touches and constant denials of hidden truths. Her days flowed into a fantasy of hallucinations concepts and visualizations. She loved the idea of having complete control of the outlook, while she hid inside her apartment that flourished with overflowing garbage, stale cigarette butts, stained dirty laundry and empty pill containers.

Her apartment smelled terrible, along with the stench of sweet, salty sweat, and sour vomit.

There were greasy cardboard pizza boxes and some left over rotten food still lying about the place. She was still wearing the green fluorescent t-shirt and khaki shorts from three days ago and hadn't showered since last Tuesday. Her brunette hair was caked in a tousled bun atop her head, a few long strands were stuck to the side of her face and the back of her neck as she sweat. She still had the old smudged mascara lodged under both eyes, giving her that raccoon attraction and her lips were now dry and cracking, making it hurt to smile. Looking through the peephole of her apartment door, she allowed no visitors anymore. They came knocking but never got in, she just looked at them through the tiny glass hole. They couldn't call her discontinued number of a phone bill that was never paid. They finally got exhausted and stayed away.

She had two uncles, an aunt and a couple of cousins on her mother's side and all her close friendships were lost. Her choices abandoned her because of her addiction and as the years passed, she found herself delving into the darkness, taking her away piece by piece. Any sense of family she had left a long time ago while she drifted into the background as a non-existent entity. Dazed and confused, her life at that time consisted of stumbling around her unkempt apartment. Time had no meaning as night and day crossed paths. Eventually she had become trapped inside her own mind, too afraid and paranoid to leave her apartment. She dared not look in the bathroom mirror, for fear of what looked back.

While her cell phone was her closest ally, her multi-colored pills were her only friends. She had to keep this phone on, if only to dial out to her only connection, to call for favors from the dealers. It should have been their names filled in across the government cheques that she received once a month, since all her money went directly over to them. Anxiously waiting for her drop off, she'd spend precious time, looking through the tiny peephole at their abstract faces.

The dealers came a-courting her as if going on a date, hooking up at the end of each month.

Having run out of funds, her hungry addiction still had to be fed just to support her habit.

She had gotten sooo tired and exhausted that now some of her days and nights consisted of finding herself taking trips to the hospital, sometimes faking illness, so that she could get a prescription for pain medications, when she couldn't afford the dealers rates in the middle of the month.

One evening, she agonized over her choices to either go back to the hospital again because the drugstores were closed or hope she could look cute enough for a dealer to make an exchange. The thought of running out of pills made her tremble with fear, she ran to the toilet and threw up.

Something was terribly wrong! Over the last couple of months, the pills weren't working as they once did before. Her stomach would churn, making her feel sick, always to the point of vomiting. She was also starting to remember now, more and more, incidences that had occurred in childhood, making it harder to hide. Ending her existence was a repeated thought.

She only stayed alive because she was too irresponsible to take her own life. Sitting alone with an overwhelming sense of loss, hopelessness and anticipation, these unanswered feelings had crept into her essence as she continued to feel weak and nauseated. While trying to make it through another hour, cramping had set into her bones. She still couldn't eat. Her appetite for food had waned and she knew that her weight loss had doubled; her insides felt all tore up.

The years of her addiction had finally run its course. She looked like a detoxified mess as she continued to fill herself up on glasses of warm water just to feel full. Her pills were no longer friendly as they forgot about her needs, and the pain of her childhood trauma had become her constant companion once again. The pills were now blocking the commitment to her high so that she couldn't feel the ecstasy any longer. Her emotions were taking on a leadership of their own while her depression stood at the windows of her mind, looking in and telling her to jump.

Scared, she broke down, sobbing uncontrollably in a fetal position. She finally conceded to her addiction, while the voice of her ego kept saying, "Go get handfuls of pretty colorful pills and just swallow them all."

After many shaking, achy sleepless and agonizing days and nights, coming into her first 12-step meeting for her seemed to be a very drastic measure to take; but somehow she got herself there. She quietly sat at the back of the room, trying to blend into the walls. Negative thoughts were swirling around her head, bubbling up inside of her, smacking her around and calling her a stupid fool and a good for nothing loser. It was very hard for her to concentrate on the speaker up at the front. Holding her head down she whispered to herself "Please stop the voices that want me dead."

She had never told her secrets to anybody about what her life entailed in order to just breathe. She didn't believe that anybody could understand what she was going through. She closed her eyes but didn't like what she saw and quickly opened them again, as she sat nervously, wringing both hands together. Her anxiety was kicking in fast, showing up in her subtle movement. God, how she wanted to throw back a few pretty pills at that moment, just to take the edge off. While sitting there, her thoughts selfishly conspired to a place of secrecy, so that she could fantasize about using just one more time. Even though she didn't fully understand the concept of, "Not using…no matter what", she acknowledged that something was happening internally to her that she couldn't exactly pinpoint. For once, she hadn't picked up, ordered or swallowed any pills, even though her mind would tell her to use. She would still catch herself daydreaming more times than not about how she could pick-up "IF" such and such were to happen.

Slowly, one by one, the self-reflecting stories of the people at the meeting would cut through and interrupt her own self-serving thoughts and she would hear them talking now about their own feelings of loss and contempt. At first, as she listened, she heard how most of them were slowly getting better and doing things that they couldn't have imagined themselves achieving, because of their past lifestyles and choices while in their own addictions. Somewhere in the room she heard the silent echoes of freedom as she was white-knuckling her quitting agenda and going it all alone. One eventful evening, while sitting in a meeting, something happened for her that started a slow growth along her recovery path. She finally found the strength to get up and speak some of her truth. Now, from somewhere, she was finding some inner strength to stand alone in front of these strangers and share her demons. She started to share what she had been living through as a child, with no understanding that she was not to blame. After she told the awful things she felt she did as a child; the feelings of blame and the anguish and resentments of not being loved, not knowing how to deal with life's blows.

Her terrible secrets that she kept hidden for so long finally came tumbling out of her. Standing in front of everyone, her whole body started to shake quietly, quickly engulfing her into the shameful feelings that she hatched from, again, badly wanting to use in that moment and take herself away. She felt naked and overexposed, but it was too late, she opened up Pandora's Box for all to finally see inside. She sat back down and was startled by the applause that they gave to her, as if she had just won a great prize. She felt more comfortable sitting, looking down at the floor. It was hard at that time to raise her head, and look at the small crowd in the church basement room.

She wasn't quite sure exactly how to feel when her embarrassment took a backseat and, in its place, she found a sense of recognition and relief. Even though tears were starting to well up at the corners of her eyes, she didn't feel like crying in that moment; she wasn't sad; instead she was feeling a sense of accomplishment and pride. As she again looked around the room, she noticed the smiles that were all directed at her, some people even asked if they could give her a hug! She still couldn't fathom why she put herself in the direct limelight of taking up air and space; only that she knew the pain of using had gotten so much stronger than the pain of living. In that moment she could identify and understand the small child within her; who had been too afraid to live in an adult world. She could start now to give herself permission to heal and get ready to take back which was stolen from her… her soul. She was no longer different from them; she lifted her head high as she received the hidden messages that she no longer had to carry the shame of the adult who used her body for his own sexual gratification and she no longer had to feel badly for trying to protect herself against the intruder who was still involved with her mother to this day.

Three months later, now experiencing "The Pink Cloud Effect" of feeling good about life in general, more months had gone by without having to use. She found that coming to a meeting every so often seemed to be helping her to stay clean, as it got her out of her apartment and she started to bathe regularly again. She even found herself going for a coffee with a few of the attendees. The only problem was nobody told her that the "Pink Cloud" effect wouldn't last and that her cravings and mind games that came with addiction world, would come back and try to bite her in the ass. With the realization that her need for using was just as strong as ever, and not knowing how the addiction works; haunting her dreams and waking hours, she assumed that she was now cured.

After a couple days of a really bad emotional setback she relapsed, then vigorously jumping back into the program again, continuing with the meetings, this time, taking suggestions and asking for assistance on staying clean, getting someone with years of recovery to help her. She had to put her ego aside, but through letting someone in she became willing. She finally discovered a feeling that she hadn't had since childhood, the feeling of courage. This was the same powerful feeling she felt the evening when she decided, that she would no longer allow her stepfather to come into her bed at night.

That night, shc would wait and pretend to be asleep and when he entered her room, she was ready for him. Wrapped up in her tiny eight year old hands, she held tight onto the sharp pencil.

The power she felt that night had quieted all her fears. When her step-father leaned his heaviness against her fragile body this time, she furiously started jabbing the air, the sharpness of the pencil lead, catching into his left eye socket. Now that same courage that she found to protect her from her step-father that night, was the same courage that brought her back to meetings night after night, to save her life. Her courage stopped her step-dad from ever entering her room again; instead he was driven to the hospital by ambulance, screaming, "My eye! My eye!" That same feeling helped her that night to protect her sanity. Afterwards she went into a shell of outward denial, while inside, she had become a broken little human being. This eventually led her to becoming a shattered adult. After that incident, her own mother would choose to stay with her stepfather, sealing her fate. This feeling of power never came to her in all her time of using. The excitement of discovery, the openness of truth and the beginning of hope was very overwhelming but beautiful at the same time. She then started to cry and this time she didn't mind the tears. She let them flow.

For the first time in many, many years she actually had real emotions that were buried so deep inside. Her fear of letting them come up drove her to a place of isolation and avoidance. She sat there quietly exploring her mind with her newfound feelings when suddenly there was a soft touch on her shoulder from behind. Her old instincts to jump up, and hide kicked in for a minute, then the gentleness of the touch brought her back to where she was, she slowly turned her head. There behind her, sat a young woman. First she thought she knew her. In a shaky quiet voice, the young girl whispered, "Thank-you". The acknowledgement and powerful recognition of two people's existence of a shared experience with suffering was both evident and vital. The young woman then asked her, "Would you mind if I sat up here with you?" Looking into that young lady's eyes at the meeting, she saw a mirror of herself, just a few months back. Introducing themselves, the two women sat silently together, listening to the others in the room speak their truths. After the meeting ended, the two of them sat and talked quietly for a while. Before parting ways, they gave each other a hug, feeling their commonness entwine. In their goodbyes they made a plan to see each other at the next meeting. She could now see her own daily growth through the young girl's eyes, as she'd meet up with her for coffee and share on how their day was going. The young girl and the 12-step program were helping her to stay clean.

Now, she really believes in a power much greater than her own, a higher power has been working in her life and she is in a position to give back because of being over a year in recovery. She knew that her own journey wouldn't be easy and through trauma therapy, she learned that because of her childhood abuse, she in turn, felt unworthy, starting the need to self-abuse.

Finally, for the first time in her life, since she was a child, she knew that life was worth living and she was worth waiting for.

Super Life

Dee Hope

Not climatized to the primary life, trials, dramas, stages
in which I played different parts,
my saga goes on another day to be reborn, forgiven; thrive,
alive
The prodigal has come home, no throne, but bones aged
by time, survived,
My true riches are not gold, this story told from my soul.
The world often cold, unknown,
supposed assumed, colorful rich and bold the truth
be told.
This is my super life. My life.

Frugal or stupid, innocent, pure, tested, procured, unsure,
secure, allured, LIFE.
The life I live, at times I love, daydreams yet to be born,
and nurtured, manifested, this I know
Who knew I would make it this far, only God can hear me
when I cry, aloud inside
Humbled mother and child, my family, the friends I love
unconditionally, personally, spiritually
in the stillness of the night I dream consistently,
holding on to love, my self,
where it is kept, the stone frame that holds my heart
mirrored, authenticated, anticipated, the prose of destiny
trying to live the super life, Super Life.
The life God has given me, every woman has the right
to be free, I am just being me

Living the edge of my persona's tribulation, I don't know,
I am not superhuman
Don't get too close to me, for you crowd my individuality,
expose my fragility
Super duper egotistical mentality, oops, I mean holistic
being, detoxing vulnerabilities
Stave off some responsibilities, for me, work and work
for mere society, not a super life at all
I am going to do it, been through it, community centered,
family oriented. Not a superwoman,
only human
Living in the now and not taking days for granted, I live
for my babies, living a single mother life
Explored it, walked it, tepidly taking a bath, whether I am
cold or hot, I didn't come with a manual.
Warranty or guarantee, natural, formidable, trying to reach
something higher than myself

I reflect on my super life. Portals of gratitude
in my mind's eye, blessings and curses massacre
my self — by survival, the sign of the times
Oh! but those unfolding possibilities and affirmed destiny,
but to one more time, try what else I can do,
Don't get caught up in human imperfection, dreams live
and die, thrive, believe to survive.
A historic orphan of circumstance, spontaneity at my back.
I look to you Lord where I stand, your
footprints in the sand.

Often strangled by rage, oh I am afraid to try again.
Self indifference can be often misconstrued,
a judgement can be cruel, chosen by God, I can't pretend,
whom all blessings flow, to SUPER
LIFE
you may burn from stern disposition
In this life, sometimes I cannot believe my eyes,
human's distaste for human beings.
Not super, destroying one's right to live their life, by strife,
unforgiveness and pride.
Born into changing times and ever changing intolerance,
I ponder with dignity and in pride.
My Super Life

Launch

Penelope Klees

Launch
Launched
Petals, Seeds
of flowers and trees
Rise and flow
into the air
Thrown
UP
and
OUT
High into the skies
By some unseen hidden hand
Scattering them
Into the wind
Mother Nature's hand

Seeds and Petals
the wind scatters them
Bright, colourful
Petals, Seeds
Bright, Oranges,
Pinks and Yellows,
Reds and Greens

Seeds of many colours
of flowers and trees
Swept up
To be

REBORN
as flowers, leaves and trees
that give
Food, Scent and Beauty
Across the Land

An Imm-Permanent Resident

Neha Poduval

A lot of girls in India want to be married to someone who's settled "Abroad!" As teenagers my girlfriends and I spent hours chatting about the kind of man we would like to marry. Wishing and hoping together to find someone living in New York, London or Toronto. A Software Engineer or an Investment Banker earning a big salary. Someone who'd take us out shopping at high-end designer stores and partying in posh clubs. These conversations would go on for hours as we giggled while downing copious amounts of chai! Most Indians naively still believe that everyone living aboard is rich and living the high life!

Though it was exciting living through these fantastical reveries, somewhere I always doubted my capabilities of living and thriving in another country. I surely dreamt of going abroad with my husband, travelling to faraway lands, meeting new people, and exploring diverse cultures; but the only difference was I wanted to come back home afterwards.

As I grew older the doubt changed into surety. I wanted to live in Mumbai. Always. I'd mock my friends who were looking for prospective husbands living abroad. But it's not their fault. Most girls back home are raised to think that way. My mother always believed that settling down abroad would be the best option for me. Her worst fear was me falling in love with a neighbourhood Romeo and living the rest of my life in the next building! She would always say, "There's nothing here for you! Find a nice boy who's settled abroad, then you can spread your wings and fly!" Fortunately for me, my parents were liberal enough to let me do what I wanted as long as I realized my potential to its fullest.

But the sad part is that most parents in India still want a bright future for their daughter only through marriage. It's the sons who are encouraged to build a career that would take them out of India. For the daughter it's always, "Do whatever you want after marriage!" As a country that's progressing at such a fast pace India still has a long way to go!

We have a family astrologer who can read palms and predict if you are destined to go abroad! According to him, there's something called the "foreign line" on your palm. You either have it or you don't. Apparently it did not exist on my hand! Imagine my mother's disappointment. At that point I reminded her that it was just last year that I had visited my aunt in Dubai. To which she promptly replied, "He means after marriage!" I was happy! I secretly believed the astrologer. I still believe in ghosts, so, ya! I was happy I wasn't going to settle abroad! I was happy I was going to stay in Mumbai, where I belonged, where I was born, where I grew up!

Mumbai is a great City! They say that once you've lived in Mumbai you can't be happy living anywhere else. I don't think there is another city in the world that stinks shitty and smells deliciously fragrant at the same time. Where overcrowded local trains annoy the life out of you, but take the road one day, and you realize you are better-off grinding sweaty bodies if you wish to get anywhere on time. Where year after year you curse the government for not unclogging the drains as you make your way through knee deep waters in the legendary Mumbai monsoons but the next moment you are marveling at the beauty of the rains as you enjoy a piping hot chai with crispy pakoras at a street side tea stall.

Mumbai is not just a city. It's an emotion! A state of being! Mumbai flows in the blood of its citizens. It's in the time that seems to have its own mind. It's in the food that nourishes you and makes you sick. It's in the sweat that drips from the brows of its citizens. The city possesses you. You are Mumbai. I was Mumbai. I never imagined leaving Mumbai. I had friends. I had family. I knew who my neighbours were and could walk into their homes as if they were mine. And because I stayed with my parents I was never lonely. I was home.

Then I fell in love and got married to the man of my dreams! Everything was perfect. He was perfect. He was also a permanent resident of Canada. He knew quite well that I wasn't keen on moving out of Mumbai and he was fine with it. He loved Mumbai as much as I did. We got married at the end of 2014 and his permanent residence card was going to expire at the end of 2015. We were blissfully happy living together in Mumbai, resigned to the idea that we weren't going anywhere. But, ironically enough, life indeed had different plans for us.

Doing theatre for a living, we were just about getting by. For the first few months of our marriage we were too dizzy gallivanting around our love horses to realize that our resources were slowly depleting. We needed to buckle up. That's when my husband suggested that maybe we should look at going to Canada. He said he could apply for a spousal sponsorship for me while he renewed his permanent residency. I could go there with him on a visitor visa so that we could still be together. He would find a job, make some money, so that we could refill our resources and I could take a couple of months off. "Look at it like a very long vacation." he said, "Once your spousal application is processed and you get a permanent residency status, we can do what we want. We can explore the theatre scene there or start all over and do something completely different. The whole world will open up for us."

This sounded very exciting and easy. But I still wasn't

very sure. There was this voice in my head telling me "No! This is not what you want". But at the same time it seemed like if I refused I would be shutting the door on a future full of endless possibilities. My husband said, "Don't over think, and let us just go! If at any point you feel like you've had enough remember that we'll always have a home here." I gave in. I agreed to go to Canada. After all what was the harm in trying? I always wanted to travel.

My husband immediately filled in the sponsorship paperwork and sent it to his family in Canada so that they could send it to the immigration board. Everything seemed fine.

We booked our flight tickets and I applied for a visitor visa through a travel agent and it immediately got rejected. It was almost like the universe was giving me a sign. Though my heart still wasn't fully convinced, I had made up my mind. I was going to Canada. I applied again, this time independently and got a six month multiple entry visit visa to Canada. I thought six months is perfect. Just enough time for a "Very Long Vacation".

It's been more than two years and counting since I came to Canada as a visitor. Since then my permanent residency application has been denied once; has been appealed for reconsideration once; has been completely withdrawn once; has been freshly reapplied for once; the fresh application has been returned back to us unprocessed once; and has been sent back by us one more time. In the meantime my visitors visa has been extended twice while I continue to wait for a complete stranger to decide whether I deserve to be a part of this country. This indeed is the future with endless possibilities, just not what we were hoping for.

We all take the luxury of permanence for granted till the carpet is swept out from under our feet. It's only when life starts to wobble and you feel like you are constantly standing on a skateboard that you realize the importance of the steady ground. If only not knowing what's going to happen next and living your life from moment to moment was as romantic and adventurous as it sounds. The words migration and immigration bring to my mind glorious images of birds and animals moving from one place to another, over sweeping skies and dramatic landscapes, in search of a better life. Shouldn't it be the same for us? Why, then, is the human immigration system so meticulously designed to invoke fear and frustration? Why is it a one-sided waiting game that seeps into the marrow of your existence; consuming lifetimes, crushing aspirations and turning dreams into stones?

I cannot leave Canada because mine is an inland application. But I also don't want to leave Canada because, in the time that I have spent in this beautiful country, I have come to love it. Though I have housed myself on this land and my heart has found a sense of belonging here, it's just a missing piece of paper that stops me from calling it home. This is the end of my story that is waiting to begin.

Fall 3

Prabha Jerrybandan

It was fall. At this time, it could be icy enough to suck out any remaining warmth, or mild enough for temptations of the living. The coldness of the world had glued her to him. Her fire had been denied so many times that she felt it had been put out for good. With tightness in her throat, and a quickness of her pulse, she pulled the frigid air into her body and pushed on. The new city was bleak. Bodies moved around without color, refusing her need for touch.

Something about the darkness of the subway tracks scared Surya. She pulled herself away from the edge as the ominous screeching of the TTC train called out to her. A wind blew her thin, black coat open – showing her faded jeans and filling her bosom with a chill.

"Why do they take so long to exit?" She thought. "I won't find a seat." Having come from Trinidad, a sun-filled place, public transport for her had been hopping into a taxi, maxi-taxi or mini buses that moved along the rough roads of the Old Southern Main Road. In so many ways, it was a backward land. People there always knew where they were going, and the distances were never too long. Commutes were always in small enough groups that everyone could at least say "Good morning." Here, she was not seen.

Surya glanced at her cellphone. Not wanting to watch, but longing to know whether Krish had called. She wanted him to call her many times. She wanted to be the one that didn't answer. Listening to a young mother talk to her young child in a stroller, she wondered about why she was so loud. The parent was talking about herself in the third person, and the baby was obviously not paying attention. In this country, parents doted on children way into adulthood. It was fashionable to do so and it made for good conversation when there was nothing pressing enough to discuss. So many things in this place grated on her.

As a child, the green-ness around her had hardly made any difference. There was so much of it. With the heat, the sky, the road, the people—she could barely breathe. She'd heard her mother repeatedly tell a story of when she was a tiny baby, and her nose was clogged with snot. To prevent her from sniffling, her mother had sucked her airways clear. These days, in a country where the starkness of white and dark loomed, Surya longed for a glimpse of life and color. She wanted to keep a flowering plant, but it would certainly die in her dark, basement apartment.

Surya got off the subway train and joined the long line of would-be passengers for the bus to the University. She was leading a tutorial for a boring education course. Barely remembering the readings she had done last night, she moved heavily towards her work for the day. One of the things she found both funny and sad, was when the students bullshitted about what they'd not read. "North Americans," she thought, "they could talk about anything." She'd come from a place that was different. Her memories of childhood floated around in her head: "Put your fingers on your lips!" The teacher's big, halfway coloured light-pink mouth would slowly form the words. The heat of the afternoon would press against the child's eyes. She imagined being older, richer and married.

For most of the time in her island home, Surya had wanted to be somewhere else. She wanted to escape the stickiness of the small town of San Fernando. Watching shows on TV, she saw herself in the big city and knew that she would go there someday. Her mother called out to her, "Did you give your brother something to eat? Did you do your school-work?"

The bus stopped at the University Commons and everyone piled out. She had resisted calling him so far; glad to be taken up in her mundane job as a T.A. Checking through her cellphone, Surya checked the last time that he'd called—it was three days ago. He'd spoken to her briefly, just as she was about to take the test. As usual, he was preoccupied with his daughter. This eighteen-year old child had been the bane of their relationship—jealous of Surya's presence in her father's life, she was always calling for his attention. They ended the conversation with strain, nothing much had really been said between them.

Surya was never sure about her relationship with Krish. She knew that the situation with him was grim for her. A single woman, a graduate student in a big city, and missing the company of people in her life, she had found it hard to leave. They had been on and off for the past two and a half years. He had chosen to live with his mother when his wife had had an affair. Surya felt that his coldness was, in part, a consequence of the matter-of-fact way in which his wife had related to him; her unfaithfulness. His mother, however, relished a man's presence in her life once more, since her husband had passed away a few years before. They were the perfect family—a man, his daughter, his mother. There was no place for another woman there.

After finishing her shift at the University, Surya took the reverse route back to her home—a grungy, basement apartment on Sheppard Avenue. She'd never lived underground before. In Trinidad, all the houses were above ground, and there was lots of sunshine and warm air. Her apartment in Toronto was always cold, even in the summer. Tired from a long day, she was aggravated further by the churning of her stomach. She had heard women talk about morning sickness. For the last week and a half, Surya had been nauseous every night. It was three days ago when she had seen the bright, blue plus sign appear, having stuck the plastic stick into a glass with her pee.

As a girl, Surya had always imagined being someone's wife. In her imagination, she had many children and she was always happy. Real life had not turned out like her imagination. She was thirty-five, single and pregnant. She didn't get much sleep that night. Her mind kept going over the conversation she wanted to have three days ago with Krish. On telling him that she was having his baby, she hoped that he would turn into the man she had wanted him to be. Their conversation had been so awkward; she decided not to tell him. Their most recent fight stemmed from his refusal to take her to a movie. His mother had insisted that he should be doing "those things" with his daughter instead.

The alarm clock was sounding louder and louder. She was hearing it but she couldn't quite tell if it was real or in her dream. Eventually rolling over to push the snooze knob on the old Westclox, she repeatedly smacked her dry lips. Her mouth felt stale and gritty; her chest felt hollow and heavy. Surya lay in her bed, pulled the blanket tighter under her chin, and tried to remember where she was, and what she was doing there.

She could barely drink any of the strong, Red Rose tea that she had made. Her stomach was still queasy from the vomiting last night. Surya showered slowly—a luxury she didn't usually have when she was rushing to her two jobs that were necessary to feed herself. She put on an old coat that she had bought on sale at Fairweather two falls before. It made her feel poor.

Looking out the window of the bus travelling south on Dufferin Street, Surya barely noticed the greyness of the day. Her face felt puffy and her breasts were tender. The bus stopped abruptly and she was glad to be shocked out of her stupor. It was her stop. She rushed out the door close behind the young man who must have pressed the "stop" button. "Thank you," she muttered to the driver. The air was dry so it felt hard to breathe in. Surya looked at the address she had written on an envelope. Her Internet bill was still inside, unpaid. Turning the corner on Lawrence Avenue, she wanted to walk the distance to the medical centre. As if it would make up her mind more, her steps were slower than usual. Flurries were beginning to fall, soft and white. Surya turned into the walkway of the "Women's Care Clinic" and thought about the new beginning she would have when she came out.

Herstory

Brittany Campbell

There are two types of women in the world: those who are born seeking the truth of who they are, and those who teach the truth of who they are.

I've been around for a very long time, watching the continuance of a matrilineal line that started with me. Women, who have never seen my face or heard my name, bear the curve of my hips and the kink in my hair. If someone had told me that I'd be spending the afterlife watching over the daughters of my descendants from behind the clouds, I would've thought they were crazy. But somehow, throughout the centuries, I have come to realize that the same way a mother is responsible for the creation of her daughter's body, I am responsible for the energy of the soul.

The women in our family had always been shunned for our strong nature. When rebellious slaves were brought to Jamaica, it was the Walker women who'd come together to lead the slaves to the hills. We possessed immeasurable strength, but wherever there is a strong woman, there is always adversity.

Sanaa was no different from the long line of distinguished, powerful women that'd come before her; I could tell from the moment that she'd opened her eyes for the first time. Bright, big and full of wonder; she'd came out of her mother knowing things already.

As a child, she'd spent her time whispering to the flowers in the garden so they would grow. On days where she walked through the Fern Gulley, she'd bowed to the towering banana trees and traced the wrinkles in their bark with her fingertips. To her, they were the majestic elders watching over the lush, tropical greenery. She spoke to the clouds and asked them to send messages to her ancestors. She pictured them smiling down on her during the days when she would lay on her back and feel every inch of her molasses skin come alive under the sun's warm kisses. She was as wild as the white wood asters that grew along the fence behind her house. A dark mystery and bewildering beauty, Sanaa's brown curly tendrils ran down her back like the waterfalls she'd danced under when no one was looking. I watched her grow, her long limbs extending like the branches of the Guango trees. Her lips permanently stained blush from the panganat she picked from her grandmother's tree.

As she grew, the innocence of how unique she was suddenly became a vulnerability in a world of despair. Her soul was the lit flame on a candle wick that I tried to shelter from the harsh winds of reality, but you see, there's only so much that I can do from the heavens. It was time. She was searching and breathlessly waiting for her world to bloom; she was ready for life.

There was always something so enchanting about the countryside in the spring months. Pollination was in the air as the bees brought the blossoms of wild flowers to life. The sun shone through the leaves of the coconut trees, providing shade for the wild hogs that reigned over the property behind the house. The mountains in the hazy distance surrounded the village as if they were separating them from the rest of the world, and as the humidity made the village slothful, old rastas, carrying bushels on their heads, scared little children as they told them stories about the duppies from the graves that arose at night.

Sanaa and her grandmother sat on the porch behind the

gate weaving baskets made out of palm leaves to sell in the marketplace in the next town over. It was their daily ritual, and while Sanaa hated the hours spent in silence weaving baskets as the busy village moved to the Calypso of the island sounds, it was their means of earning money. Sanaa much rather enjoyed running through the jungle chasing after hummingbirds, but she was constantly reminded that, "good women learn in quietness and full submission," as her grandmother always said.

Ms. Maisie, as most of the village referred to her, raised Sanaa since she'd been a baby. She was the village's medicine woman who'd devoted her time to helping the villagers with everything from a toothache to a broken heart. Sanaa could remember her grandmother mixing floral concoctions together to make love potions for women who were desperate to make a man fall in love with them. She even remembered her grandmother stirring mud over the fire for a man who needed his crops to grow during the big drought. Whether it was a parasite from the soil in her garden, like the doctor said, or a curse for dabbling in witchcraft, like the village believed, Ms. Maisie had lost her sight when Sanaa was six and since then, she hadn't been the same. To her, losing her sight was a curse that she had to endure for being a woman who didn't know her place.

"Mischief come by di pound and go by di ounce." Ms. Maisie would say, warning Sanaa about living life in the clouds.

Presently, it felt as if the roles were reversed. Sanaa became the caregiver, while her grandmother's health deteriorated. As Sanaa weaved her fifth basket for the day, a strong breeze from the mountains blew by slightly brushing against her damp skin. It was as if the wind was lifting her head to watch him walk past her gate. The men around the village mostly worked up at Conna's farm, harvesting pimento to sell at the marketplace in the city. They were all rugged and parched at the end of each day as they made their way to the nearby shop for a drink. Among the crowd of tired men was Bevardo, a brooding afro-latin boy wrapped up in a dark, mostly silent, melancholia.

Almost tripping over her linen white dress, Sanaa ran up to the gate and rested her chin on her forearms as she called out to him. "Bevardo Beech, I made me some cybill orange juice if you'd like to come by and try some."

Bevardo smiled, tilted his hat, and kept walking with the crowd. Bevardo and Sanaa grew up together in the village. When they were children he'd been her partner in crime. They'd jumped into rivers and climbed mango trees together. On hot days they'd laid in the tall grasses stealing innocent kisses from each other, while the old heads went about their day selling items in the market. Sanaa wasn't sure what changed, but as Bevardo grew into a man, he was discouraged from talking to her. It seemed as if she was too outlandish to be associated with him.

Sanaa walked backwards to her seat on the porch, her gaze still stuck on Bevardo as he disappeared into the crowd of men walking through town.

"You shake a man's hand, you don't shake his heart."

Sanaa shot a frustrated look back at her grandmother. She always had a comment about who Sanaa was and today was the last straw. Ms. Maisie had become like a sheep following the standards of the other people in the village, but Sanaa had come alive with the nature of the jungle, and she yearned to be noticed.

As dusk fell onto the village streets, Sanaa put her grandmother to bed early, ran some cold water over her face, and pinned back her heavy tresses as she made her way to the tin roof shop where she knew she could find what she was looking for. Her dress was thin and loose, not like the other women who wore layers of fashionable garments in various colours. As she walked down the street in the moonlight, the silhouette of her lean legs was outlined beneath her dress.

As she approached the tin roof shop, Sanaa could smell the thick musk of smoke and sweat from the men who sat around the entrance of the shop drinking rum and playing dominoes on small rickety tables.

"Good evening," she said softly as she made her way through the shop's entrance. Walking through the room was like walking through quicksand. Not one soul moved out of Sanaa's way as she looked around for a glance of Bevardo.

"Girl, don't you know that women aren't allowed in the shop when we're drinking?" one man said as he took a big gulp of brandy from a rusty steel cup. Sanaa ignored his comment and stood on the tip of her toes to see above the crowd.

Just then, she felt a tight grip around her arm and suddenly she was being pulled out of the shop and into the street.

"Get your filthy hands off of me!" she screamed as she looked back to see who it was.

Bevardo smirked and motioned with his hands to calm down, "You are too much," he said as he let go of her arm and placed his hands in his pockets.

He was tall and lean. Now that he was a man, Sanaa could see where his cheeks were once soft and plump were now chiseled and full of coarse facial hair. "Care to walk me home?" Sanaa said in whispered tones.

Bevardo chuckled and shook his head, " Sanaa you nuh easy, you came all the way down here just to get me to walk you all the way back home?"

Sanaa coyly smiled and grabbed Bevardo's hand from his

pocket and skipped off into the darkness, pulling him behind her.

The country roads were pitch black with only the moonlight guiding the way. Sanaa was in utter bliss, this was the first time that a man had ever walked her home and the fact that it was Bevardo made it an even better occasion. Through heavy laughter and glances, Bevardo managed to walk Sanaa home before the kerosene street lamps went out. By the entrance of her grandmother's gate, Bevardo gazed into her eyes; he brushed a curl away from her forehead before gently pressing his lips on to hers.

"I'm sorry. May I kiss you?" Bevardo whispered in her ear.

Sanaa nodded and leaned into him. Their bodies pressed against each other so close that Sanaa was sure that Bevardo could feel her heart thumping through her chest. Once again Bevardo placed his hand around the small of her arm and firmly gripped it as he kissed her again.

Sanaa had always pictured this exact moment when she'd been a little girl. Kissing Devardo seemed like a dream, but like most dreams, she knew with one small instance it could become a nightmare.

He tightened his grip around her arm, and his kisses were now hard and rough. Suddenly Sanaa's choice felt like a trap.

"Bevardo, Bevardo, I think I'm going to head inside now." Sanaa said breathlessly, but his grip only tightened around her arms, almost numbing her hands.

"Bevardo, stop!" Sanaa had begun to pull away, but he'd already begun to pull her into the darkness behind the house, where Sanaa had spent her time laying under the blossoming pear trees.

And just like that, engulfed in the darkness of the jungle

that she knew so well, Sanaa became a prisoner. With one hand covering her mouth and the other pushing her face first into the wet grass, Sanaa knew that the Bevardo who she used to skip rocks with by the river had disappeared.

"Stay still and keep quiet." His breath felt hot and stale against her face. His hands, which she once held while walking to primary school, were now crawling all over her like insects. His fingers curled up inside of her, exploring places that he was denied access to. She grew tired of fighting back, she fixated on a rotting pear that had fallen from the tree nearby as Bevardo ripped the bodice of her white dress and invaded the space between her legs.

The moment was so sudden. The line between choice and misfortune blurred somewhere between Bevardo's sweet kisses and the brutal attack.

"Remember you wanted this, you pursued me." He said as he fumbled with the buttons on his pants. He stood up glaring down at Sanaa who was paralyzed in fear. "Maybe next time you'll behave like a lady."

A woman's story is never monolithic. It is like the ocean, moving in harsh tides or small rhythmic waves, and different on every shore. I could continue Sanaa's story simply by telling you that this is a story of love and loss. I could tell you how Bevardo paid for what he did, and how the village forever blamed her for her own assault. But instead I'll tell you about the story of her soul.

That night, a part of Sanaa died. The innocence that she'd perceived the world through had deteriorated. Laying face first in the cold wet grass, Sanaa could hear the sound of his heavy footsteps move further away from her limp body.

The sun began to peek up from the darkness, and, as the

sky started to lighten, Sanaa draped her tattered dress around her body, fearing that someone would walk past her and see her shame. Everything about who she was shaken to the core, her insides became numb to the senses in her body that used to bring her such pleasure in life. Everything in her called out to the wild for solace, but all she could feel was silence. She walked into the darkness of the jungle as if she was running from the light of the rising sun behind her; her feet damp and cut up from the sticks and stones that felt like cement.

She ran to the edge of the river that ran through the Fern Gulley and collapsed to her knees in a clearing of dirt and moss. Every corner of the jungle rang out in despair as Sanaa mourned the girl that she used to be.

Among the echoes of her sobbing, there was a finished silence. Suddenly the jungle was so still and calm that for the first time that night, she could hear the wind stir the leaves and the world awaken from its deep slumber. It was another day.

By now, the sun had caught up to Sanaa and as it rose, illuminating everything in its path, the river began to glisten. Sanaa inched her way to the edge of the river where the natural springs between the rocks pumped fresh water into the stream.

In her reflection she could see the bruises on her face and the dirt that encased her body, but in her eyes she could see a glimpse of the small flame that needed to be nurtured deep within her soul. Of course Sanaa's soul wasn't dead, she could never truly be dead until she'd finished feeling, thinking and experiencing. She realized that just like the jungle, among the darkness, there was peace.

Once the dusk turned into dawn, Sanaa made her way back to her grandmother's house. She stepped through the door and found her grandmother sitting on her rocking chair, fretful about her late return home.

"Lawd child, where were you?" Ms. Maisie breathed out heavily, "Out all hours of the night! Don't you know a soldier's blood is the general's reputation?"

Sanaa closed the door behind her and leaned up against it with both feet planted firmly on the ground.

"Ms. Maisie, nuh need to worry about where I was and who I will be. I was out in the world finding out about living."

I Believed He Was Coming Home

Christina Walsh

In mid-August 1999, I met my psychiatrist Dr. Larry Williams. He was referred to me by my family doctor. His office was located at 402 Parliament Street, in Toronto, at the back of a pharmacy. I remember how we clicked instantly. I remember telling him how much I needed time to work through difficult issues relating to severe post-traumatic stress.

"I'll give you the 75 minute appointments, vs. the 45 minute ones since you are worth it. I can see you 3-4 times a week," Dr. Williams said to me.

I liked hearing that. I liked how much he appreciated my dedication to come to therapy, despite it being difficult many times. He dealt with many rough cases in Regent Park, and I was one of them. I was relieved to have someone to talk to, someone to help me work through my issues. I was blessed.

Two weeks had passed, and Dr. Williams' secretary called, saying, "Dr. Williams is in the hospital, he won't be back for a while."

"When will he be back?" I gasped.

"I'm not sure."

"Tell me where he is," I pleaded.

"He's at Wellesley Hospital"

I hung up the phone and cried uncontrollably for three hours. I finally rushed to see him.

"Can I see Larry Williams?" I said at the front desk, "I'm a friend of his."

"No, he's not accepting visitors"

"Give him this card I made for him, please."

"We will."

I left crying, numb, scared for him.

Four grueling months had passed, and Dr. Williams finally returned to work. I was relieved. We resumed our therapy sessions. "I barely eat enough," I said.

"I'll take you to the joint up the street and treat you to some home cooking," Dr. Williams said. "I want to teach you to eat well, and to make sure you're fed." We had some of our sessions at that joint, keeping them light.

I was moved that he wanted to teach me social graces, as well as regular eating habits. Nobody had taught me that before. At times, he got us pizza from Dominos.

I liked his generous spirit. "I'll give you this dictionary, so you can improve your vocabulary" he said, handing me an old Webster's dictionary. We spent many sessions going through some of the dictionary. I felt like I was in school, with a teacher who cared about me, finally.

Over a year had passed. I arrived at session one morning, noticing two new green recliners in his office. "One of these is for you to sit in, since you told me you love recliners" Dr. Williams said. I was floored. "Someone actually remembered what I liked," I thought to myself.

"Meet my dog, Bagel the beagle," Dr. Williams said during another session. Bagel took to me; he sat in my lap. He had deep brown eyes like my doctor's. "He cried when you left yesterday," said Dr. Williams. "You were the only one he cried after. He didn't care for anyone else."

It was now March, 2002. "Let's have our sessions in the Bloor/Bathurst area, closer to my home at a coffee shop," Dr. Williams offered.

"Sure," I replied. For the next two months, we had our sessions at Second Cup and Burger King. They were our new joints. He bought me two sandwiches now each time we met.

But somehow I sensed something wasn't quite right.

Friday, May 10, 2002, 3:45 pm. Like all encounters with Dr. Williams, I remember this one clearly. I went to see him. He was tired, and looked not like himself, not well. But I was sure I felt worse. "I had a rough night last night," I told him. "I was brought to the hospital by the police because I threatened to end my life."

"I'm sorry you went through that," he replied. We talked. The last thing he said to me that afternoon was, "See you around" Those three words, exactly. No more, no less.

A little over a week later, a Tuesday morning, my phone rang. It was my friend, Diane. "Your doctor is missing," she said. "His poster is all over the west end of the city. He's considered to be at risk." I went numb, but then immediately defiant. I believed he was missing, but I didn't believe anything about him being at risk. It was impossible. I believed he was coming home.

He didn't come home.

On May 23, 2002 -- a Thursday night -- the body of Dr. Larry Williams was found in a storage room in the apartment building where he lived. He had apparently committed suicide. All the times he had been away from work, including that first mysterious absence, suddenly fell into place.

But I prefer to remember him sitting across from me in his favourite joint, telling me to eat, making sure I stayed healthy, teaching me how to enjoy a meal with someone I could call my friend.

I think he would have preferred that, too.

Broken

Jose Mario Moreira de Oliveira

Harry was sipping beer at his favourite pub waiting for his best friend Ulysses to join him. Normally, when those things combined, beer and his friend, nothing could bring him down, but today was different. A quick look at him and you could see it: greasy hair, stained t-shirt, sweat pants and eyes swollen by crying and lack of sleep.

Ulysses finally arrived. He was almost the exact opposite of Harry; dressed to kill, charismatic and looking as fresh as youth itself.

“Hey man! What’s up?” Ulysses asks with a jolly and firm slap on his friend’s arm.

Harry nods and moans.

“Well, I’ll take the fact that you’re out of the house as progress. But you look pretty down, have to admit.”

“You think?” Harry retorts, a mix of boredom and anger.

Ulysses laughs, he’s missed his friend, even his rudeness is endearing: “Come on, dude! Man up! She’s gone, that sucks, but what you’re gonna do? Blame yourself forever? No use crying over spilled milk. Move on!”

Harry looks amused and irritated by his friend’s stupidity: “No use crying over spilled milk?” he states angrily— “If we don’t cry over spilled milk, what else will we cry for? Of course there’s no use crying , but that’s not why we cry.”

“Well, why then?”

“Why? Cause we can’t help it! The irreversibility of the spilled milk that’s the saddest thing there is. The ultimate proof of our impotence in the face of life.”

“Dude, come on! It’s just an exp…” But Harry interrupts, lifting his index finger near Ulysses’ face: “It means knowing that the destroyed love will never bloom again. That the word said in anger will not be forgotten, that the disgusting errors of the past will never be completely washed away."

As Harry says that, his anger fades into sadness and by the end of his statement, he is quietly looking at his beer, as if the answers for it all were dancing in the bubbles.

Ulysses moves to the other side of the table and hugs his friend, but Harry does not hug him back. "It will get better. I promise. That's how life works, right?"

"Life is death and destruction. The beautiful is always cruelly corrupted by time and chaos."

"Not necessarily!" Ulysses defends, "As people, we have the gift of changing, of making our own destiny! Of improving ourselves!"

"I don't think we have any gift, man. We have only the rebellious slavery of living life as powerless as any other creature, but we deceive ourselves by believing we are special and that we have some control over the order of the universe."

"Well, if you are right, then being optimistic does not make one plus one more than two, but being pessimistic does not make it less."

Harry thinks for a second and then nods at his friend, and finally hugs him back. He smiles, "Maybe happy people aren't complete idiots after all."

The two best friends laugh as the waitress brings Ulysses another beer. He moves back to the other side of the table raising his glass:

"Things are what they are, happiness and sadness come and go and what can we do? We cry over the spilled milk, but we also enjoy the beer we drink. Cheers, buddy!"

Life Of Lilies

Ana Dinar

The Lilies lined up ever so lovely,
Smelling lively, hanging loosely,
And laughing about the time that they were but
mere buds,
needing so much attention and care.
While whistling winds washes their wayward leaves,
Their petals now have puddles of pounding rain
that fell upon them.

Fearing that this is the end friends, we may never see
each other again.
But the sun shined the next day
still breathing, beautiful, bountiful air
Feeling fresh and fantastic,
for the struggles that they feared, led to survival.

From our servant that kept us safe, totally satisfied
we smiled while doing a dance called salsa.

We all stand together
run 'til we wither away,
be seeing you some time next year.
Where the growing process piles us up
to make profounding perfume
for the people around the world to remember us
as we were.

For who shall shower all of us with splendoring love.

Oh Beauty

Roberta Taylor

Root to branch to sky
  the pushing through
  to open up everything
      infinite
Light, air, space,
      being
And I will someday
  see the creator (of everything, including God)
      and I will grope
Towards heaven
    and be
    washed
      in
        beauty.

What Wispy Tendril

Jake Allderdice

I don't know if it was the sound of a train in the distance that put me in a melancholy mood, or if I was already feeling blue and the train song only underscored my mood of loss and loneliness, but in any case there I was, a useless, staring, lump of blah, searching through the evening-time window as if in the twiggy tree branches out there I'd find the answer.

But the branches held nothing for me. All they held was a shredded white plastic grocery bag. It jerked sluggishly at the end of a maple twig. If that bag were me I'd do the same; I'd be all "What's the point," I'd give up fighting. Maybe a bigger wind would come and blow me free, or maybe not. I wouldn't care. What could I do about it?

As I stared into the twilit evening, the shadows on the limp plastic bag took form, and as the bag twisted at the end of its twig it looked a little like a disembodied head, with deep-set eye sockets, a low, beetled forehead and a downturned mouth agape, whether in anguish or pain I could not say.

Then a breeze lifted the bag just a little, and I felt its face turn toward mine. I felt it looking at me, its bleak eyes locked on my own.

What was it thinking, that lifeless sac? The train whistle lowed from the city line and empty boxcars clattered across a long high bridge, and did this plastic bag of nothing, stranded atop a maple tree outside my window, did this bag look back at me and wonder what wispy tendril held me so fast? Did it pity me as I pitied it?

Transplant From Andromeda

Hildegard Gmeiner

Foreword

I am writing this book because I would like my four children to know about the experiences I had with extra-terrestrials during my early thirties, when my boys were still tiny and before my daughter was even born. It's important to me that they hear about what I lived through and how those events shaped the mother I have become to them.

I was a stay-at-home mother with three little boys under the age of five at the time, when the cause for my body unexpectedly collapsing couldn't be found, nor would the drugs given make a difference. During these out-of-body experiences, I spent time in a world of bright light, with intelligences from a neighboring galaxy. Their input and guidance were instrumental in me becoming the mother I was for my now four, grown children. This book tells my story, the way I experienced it.

Over the years I have met quite a few individuals who have had experiences with off-planet intelligence also. I believe there is a strong probability that there may be thousands, even hundreds of thousands, of similar experiencers around the world. It is in solidarity with them that I am writing this book. May it encourage others to step up and speak about their experiences also.

Another reason for writing this book is a promise I made twenty-five years ago to, yes, the Andromedan Council , specifically to one Andromedan named LuiMar. I promised LuiMar that I would write and speak about my experiences, as soon as

I had regained my health and had succeeded in raising my children. [1]

I'm very aware of how this may sound to many of you. It's possible – probable – that you might be tempted to close this book at this point and move on to something else. Still I would like to make a request. Please, hear me out. Listen to my story with the story-listening instincts you have as a human being – which are formidable to say the least.

If at any point my story bores you or strikes you as too far-fetched for your taste, by all means, close the book. However, if you find yourself engaged, even intrigued, please resist the conventional reaction of our modern western culture to explorations of alternate consciousnesses, and stay with me to the end. If it helps, imagine you're reading a work of fiction; let's say science-fiction or inspirational fiction. That is always a reader's prerogative. Yet, do bear in mind as you do, what Canadian author Charles de Lint once wrote:

"There's no such thing as fiction…If you can image something, then it's happened."

Which is exactly what an Andromedan would say. You couldn't think it, if it didn't already exist somewhere.

This book is a collection of events which actually did happen in my life.

As Dr. John E. Mack, professor of psychiatry at Harvard

---

[1] *Andromedan Council is a governing body of the Galaxy of Andromeda consisting of 12 members, each representing a specific area of the closest neighboring galaxy to the Milky Way, of which Earth is but a tiny part. The distance from Earth to Andromeda Galaxy by conventional Earth-style measuring techniques is about 2.5 million light years (1 light year = approximately 6 trillion miles)*

University showed in his book "Passport to the Cosmos", things do happen regularly to people which explode the commonly accepted norms and reference points of society. He argued that 'Experiencers' are just that, people experiencing paranormal occurrences. They ought to be listened to, not judged or belittled, which has been my experience in the past also. Dr. Mack was convinced experiencers did not necessarily need the care of a psychiatrist, just someone tolerant enough to listen to them.

Some scientists are also experiencers, which has dramatically impacted how they see their respective fields, just as my experiences completely reshaped my life.

The worldview of most people today is still largely governed by Newtonian principles, which hold that the universe is a strictly material phenomenon, governed by immutable physical laws. However, that view has been under siege, scientifically, since the early 20th century, when, the advent of quantum mechanics and Werner Heisenberg's ideas about the 'Uncertainty Principle' presented an astonishing alternative. We might not be living in a material universe with seemingly unrelated parts.

From a subatomic perspective, what once was believed to be solid particles now appears as an ocean of energy waves. It is impossible to predict when and how a waveform collapses and for a particle to materialize, though scientists believe the consciousness of an observer impacts on what materializes from a waveform. The possibilities of materialization are many, and a consciousness observing the wave might ultimately bring about a very specific manifestation. The act of observation seemingly brings about the collapsing of the wave function. For example, observing the movements of billiard balls on a table influence their behaviors.

Somehow our consciousness interacts with the field of endless possibilities, bringing about situations, which go beyond what our logical mind is capable of accepting as possible. Yet when the same situation is viewed from a quantum level perspective, all solids and waves are united in consciousness. What we once thought of as magic can now be understood as an innate, invisible, all-binding force.

In fact, a century after Heisenberg, many physicists, mathematicians, biologists, chemists, geneticists, psychotherapists and psychiatrists themselves, due to having had para-normal experiences themselves, are shifting the way they do science. Many agree such an inexplicable force does indeed exist, through which each one of us is shaping the material world. There appears to be a willingness to relinquish the notion of human insistence for "logical" control over the world in exchange for an alternate possibility of there being a collective spirit, which binds and connects all creation, whereby the material world can be influenced by the immaterial thoughts of an observer. Mysticism of old and science appear to begin to speak a similar language.

Chief Seattle, the distinguished 19th century Squamish indigenous tribal leader, who lived in the northwest coastal region of the North American continent, (the City of Seattle was named after him) explained this 'Force' by saying in his famous 'Sacred Web of Life Speech':

"The Earth doesn't belong to man; man belongs to the Earth."

Steven Hawking, the renowned British physicist, was inspired by the idea of this unknowable and invisible force also. I believe he spoke about the same force, when he developed the hallmark theory that today is the equal of Quantum Theory, the Unified Field Theory, also known as String Theory.

String Theory suggests everything in the universe, including time and space is interconnected. Everything constitutes points on a string, from which ultimately the whole fabric of creation is woven.

It's therefore very possible this fabric also connects us to intelligences from beyond our Earthly dimension.

I am not an expert, nor am I a prophet, nor am I the owner of an exclusive key to unlocking the mysteries of the universe, of life and to happiness. I am just a point on the string, a small piece in the big universal puzzle. I consider it my personal responsibility to my children and all those willing to listen, to tell the story which lies between the pages of this book. In doing so, I trust I am completing my unique puzzle piece and my purpose for being here on Earth at this time.

The story begins in spring of 1992, ten months after my youngest son was born. It ends with a day in June 2016, when I spoke about these experiences with the Andromedans for the very first time in decades to hundreds of people at the Cosmic Alien Expo in Brantford, Ontario/Canada.

(https://aliencosmicexpo.com)

You can read this story in any way that's most amenable to you. You may want to read it as a parable, a metaphor, or as an inspirational science-fiction tale.

It also happens to be my life.

Jemmy And Pip

Ken Rosser

When they got home she was sent to her room, and locked in. Though she bit her lip, cried, but muffled it with her pillow. Why did her mom have to be so mean? She hadn't been allowed to give invitations to her friends for her birthday. She could hear her parents arguing about her downstairs.

Earlier that day Jemmy and her mom had stopped in front of the toy shop in the mall. There were cars and trains, robots and bulldozers, but what stopped them were four dolls, all similar, but for their dresses and tresses. They looked like a family.

"Which one would you like for your birthday?" mom asked, but Jemmy's eyes were elsewhere.

"Don't want a doll," she said,

"Oh come now, Jemmy, when I was growing up I had dozens of dolls and teddy bears, and even toy puppies and kitties!"

Jemmy looked into her mother's eyes, "Can we get a real puppy?"

"No." her mother replied, "Dogs are too much work, and they need a lot of training."

"I can do it," Jemmy insisted. "Judy has two dogs and they know all sorts of tricks. I'm sure Judy could help."

"No dogs," her mother said with finality. "Wouldn't you rather have a doll?"

Jemmy crossed her arms and pouted. She did not want a doll, but when her mother got like this, all that mattered was what mom wanted.

"How about the one with the red hair?" Mother suggested.

Jemmy said something under her breath.

"What was that? I didn't hear it. If that was a bad word,

we're going home right now, and you'll do without supper, and a birthday present!"

"Fiiiine," said Jemmy, and she thought to herself, "I'll still be ten."

She could never win. Her mother didn't know her, her father didn't know her, and they didn't try in the least to find out her likes, or who she even was. She wasn't sure who she was either, but she was not a toy for her family to push around, and store in her room when she was being inconvenient. No birthday party? That was just the latest hurt.

It seemed like she was always in trouble. She repainted the pink frames of her glasses blue, at Danielle's house

Her parents were outraged, and said they could've killed her. They didn't want to risk using turpentine on her glasses, and new frames would be expensive, so her father said, "Well, you'll just have to live with those."

Jemmy was okay with that.

When her parents were getting the house repainted, Jemmy took a different route home after playing so she could pick out a colour at the hardware store.

"Mom! I know what colour I want!" she pulled the card out of her pocket and proudly showed a sky blue, "Number A26-6-0594-0!"

"Those weren't on sale."

"Oh?"

"Never mind, you'll love what we picked out for you."

The house was beige everywhere but her room. She rolled over and looked at the ceiling, and its unrelenting grey, like a gathering storm, or a deep dull subterranean cave. The only bright spot was her window, but it only looked out on the red brick wall of the house next door. It had taken her a while to figure out that there was a reason her parents let her pick a colour. They didn't care what she wanted.

She had some books, and she started rereading *The Wind in the Willows*, because she liked Ratty, Mole, Badger, and silly Mr. Toad.

Mom worried that she wouldn't grow up to be a proper young lady. Well, she didn't want to be a lady, she wanted to race in Toad's motorcar.

She heard the doorbell, and her mother answered. She recognized the voice, it was her dad's sister, crazy aunt Beatrice. This would be interesting. When Aunt Beatrice got loud, she was an unstoppable force of nature.

She heard the stairs creak. There was a rattle as her door was unlocked, and Aunt Beatrice came in and snatched the key from her father's hand, closed the door, and locked them both in, before putting her oversized handbag on the floor.

"Now we can have a private talk," Aunt Beatrice whispered, sitting in her desk chair, while she sat on the edge of her bed.

"Just because your parents say you can't have a birthday party, doesn't mean you won't have a party! I'll pick you up next Wednesday, and we'll go the Continental. You can order anything you want, and don't worry about your parents (she nodded toward the door), "I'll phone them to tell them where we are. I have as much of the story as your mother would give, so I know you don't want a doll. You can invite your friends, and if your friends' parents want to confirm, just give them my card."

"Okay," Jemmy said, trying not to sound as sad as she felt.

Aunt Beatrice rose and unlocked the door quietly, then wrenched it open, and her parents both fell over, "Get enough of an earful? Why don't we have a little family party while we're all here?"

Aunt Beatrice made sure Jemmy could get out of her room, and they ordered Chinese food, even though dad looked sour at having to pay for it, especially the tip her aunt insisted on.

Her parents expected Wednesday, but Aunt Beatrice was there to pick her up on Monday, thus sneaking the party right under her parents' noses.

Jemmy's favourite gifts were books. She had a boxed set of The Lord of the Rings from Aunt Beatrice that she couldn't wait to start. Billy brought her a toy race car, and she imagined Mr. Toad driving it. She'd find a special place for it. Her friends all knew she couldn't have cartoons, because her parents said they rotted the mind.

Aunt Beatrice said there was one more present and pulled a plush toy ferret from her handbag, "This was my special friend that kept me company in my loneliest days. I could tell it anything, and it never made me feel weak, wrong, or small."

"What's its name?" Jemmy asked.

"That's for you to decide. Just because it was my best friend, doesn't mean you need exactly the same friend."

Jemmy took the toy, and looked at it with a child's expert eye, "It's had some stitching up, so it must be real special. I think I'll call it Patches, no, wait, I think his name is Pip."

Pip made the rounds between the meal, and the arrival of the birthday cake, and was approved by all.

"Thank you, Aunt Beatrice, this is the best party ever!"

"Your parents said you can't be polite! All one has to do is talk to you as an equal."

When Jemmy got home, dad said he remembered Pip as something Aunt Beatrice used to carry everywhere.

Mom offered to "Throw that tatty thing away," but Jemmy hugged it tight, and declared that if they touched it, she would tell Aunt Beatrice. That stopped them.

That night, Jemmy was going to toss Pip in with her other toys, but changed her mind, and let him share her bed. The dreams that came were wilder and more exciting than any she remembered. Pip told her about the country he came from, where the trees flew, and could turn upside down so their roots could catch the rain. There were animals that lived in the trees, and voyaged all over the world, and then there were the birds that did not know up from down. There were flowers, some of which walked, and others were like butterflies, except they spun as they flew.

"I know Aunt Bea said you would talk to me when you were ready, but I didn't think it would be out loud!"

"Of course I talk out loud, how else would you hear me?"

"Could you talk to my parents?"

"I could, but we know they wouldn't listen."

"It would be great to see the looks on their faces, though."

When Jemmy woke the next morning, she had an exotic flower that glowed yellow and green in her hand as a reminder that it was more than just a dream. She put it away on her bookshelf, where she liked to display her treasures.

One day, Jemmy came home from playing with her friends, to find her parents sitting quietly at the kitchen table.

Mom started, "Aunt Beatrice is gone."

"Gone? Gone where?"

Dad continued, "Where busybody relatives go. She had a stroke last night, and passed away."

"Oh no, not Aunt Bea!"

"I'm afraid it is. You'll want to dress nice for the funeral."

Then her parents left the room, but she could hear them, say, "How do you expect her to grow up if we're always holding her hand?"

Jemmy ran to her room and closed the door where she tearfully told the news to Pip. At dinner, Jemmy wasn't able to eat much, even when reminded that there were starving children all over the world.

Her parents waited till she was out visiting friends, then took her toy chest and donated it all to Value Village.

When Jemmy came home, she was upset that she couldn't find her toys, or Pip.

Dad said it was time to put away childish things.

Jemmy was inconsolable, but quieted down soon after she went to bed. Her mother looked in on her to see that Pip was back in his accustomed place.

"Didn't we throw away all her toys? Because that Pip thing is in bed with her!"

"Impossible!"

The next day her parents turned her room upside down, but they couldn't find Pip. When night came and everything was quiet, Jemmy rescued Pip from the hall closet.

She was woken up early the next day, before she could hide Pip.

Mom said, "This old toy is carrying who knows how many germs!"

That evening, Jemmy was pining for Pip, when she saw him peeking out of her closet. She made sure he stayed hidden until her lights were turned out. She took Pip to bed, and talked silently to him, "Why do my parents have to be so mean, Pip?"

"They're trying hard, but it's difficult to tell them that their best isn't very good."

"You'll have to find a hiding place before my folks wake up, so they don't take you away again."

"I'll do my best Jemmy. You know that no matter what, I'm never far away."

"It's so awful here Pip. Do you think we should run away?"

"Run to where? I wish Aunt Bea was still around."

"I do too, Pip, I do too."

School began two weeks later, and there was Show and Tell once a week. Jemmy brought Pip, hidden in one of her parents' old briefcases. Pip was a hit with her teacher and classmates, but it was possible her parents might hear of it.

Then Jemmy got sick at school, and the nurse sent her home early with a note telling her parents that they should get Jemmy to the nearest hospital. Her parents barely looked at the note, and sent her to bed. The only one who consoled her was Pip.

The next day she was worse. She was allowed to sit up in the evening to watch a movie with her parents. As usual, it was an art house movie that she could make no sense of, but the fever she was running made it seem hilarious. The third day, she was brought to the doctor's office, where she was given a prescription for tinctures, and infusions, along with hot lemonade and eucalyptus tea, and if she was restless, add some brandy or rum.

On the way home Jemmy's mother said, "I wish you wouldn't make up symptoms in front of the doctor."

Jemmy's voice came out in a squeak, "But I didn't!"

The fourth day, her parents had tickets to TIFF so they brought in Jemmy's favourite babysitter, "Alicia from down the street."

Mom gave Alicia a note for Jemmy's care, "We believe in alternative medicine, and don't get her excited. If she asks for Pip, say you can't find it," and then they were gone.

Alicia brought some board games to Jemmy's room, "What would you like to play?"

"I don't feel well," Jemmy said, "I hurt all over."

Alicia touched Jemmy's forehead, "Man, you're hot! Did your parents leave any medicine, like for pain or anything?"

"No. I want Pip, he makes me feel better."

"What's that? Pip? Your parents said you shouldn't have Pip... But if he's that important to you."

"I hid him in the closet, but I can't move to get him."

Alicia found Pip under the towels and brought him to Jemmy, "Your folks say their phones will be off while they watch movies. There's nothing useful in this note at all!"

Alicia touched Jemmy's brow again then pulled out her cell and dialed 911 "Hello, emergency?"

The Paramedics and the Fire Department arrived and quickly bundled Jemmy into the ambulance. Alicia rode in the back, holding Pip so Jemmy could see him.

It was hours later that Jemmy's parents came home to a dark and silent house. A police officer was waiting to tell them which hospital Jemmy was in, and to turn their phones back on.

Jemmy was in intensive care, where Pip wasn't allowed, so Alicia kept hold of him while she paced the waiting room, hoping for good news.

Jemmy's parents arrived three hours later and had to tell the doctors about Jemmy's symptoms, and what medications she was on, and what her temperature was.

"We didn't take her temperature," mom said, "Because we believe in holistic druidic medicine. We blame that toy, Pip."

The doctor looked at Pip in Alicia's arms, and said, "She wouldn't have gotten this type of infection from that."

The policeman said, "We're charging you for failing to provide the necessities of life. You know what that means?

You have the right to contact your lawyer, or we will give you the number of a lawyer referral service. I caution you not to say anything, as it might be used against you in court. You understand, right?"

"You can't arrest us!" dad said, "We have to make funeral arrangements!"

"Children are such a bother," mom said, "I don't know why we even tried."

"There's another matter we are looking to talk to you about; the toxicology report on your late sister Beatrice."

"Toxicology?" dad said, "We didn't authorize an autopsy!"

"Autopsies are done every time there is a suspicious death. Now, I have to tell you not to say anything more."

"This is outrageous!" mom said. "We'll sue you for false arrest!"

To read more of JEMMY AND PIP's adventures visit: www.torontowriterscollective.ca

Greengirl

Ana Dinar

Hi! My name is Greengirl; there was a time in my life when I really hated my name and wondered why my parents had given me such a cruel name? For every single day at school, I was bullied, spat on, objects thrown at me, so tormented, that I wished never to return. The principal, Mr. Bottom, did nothing to ensure my safety, even after Barbara Britney Bungalow threw a rock that hit my left temple. I almost lost my eye. "This has got to stop!"

So I wrote a letter to our local MP, Mr. Brian Brown. I poured my heart out into that paper, and told him everything that was happening at the school and the cruel treatment that my classmates made me suffer. "Going to school is hell, but I do it, despite the fact that they're getting to me. Deep down inside, at the very core of my existence, I hate them and secretly want them to suffer," and signed it, sincerely, Greengirl.

Two weeks flew by quickly and nothing came. But on a Tuesday morning, I received a letter from our MP. He mentioned that he would put a stop to all of the suffering.

The next day, he came to school. Reporters surrounded him asking questions, photographers were taking pictures, cameramen were filming everything. I was interviewed by one lady reporter. She asked if I'd provoked them into doing terrible things.

"No!" I shouted. "I DID NOT. They don't like me because of my name."

My parents were at the school too. My mother walked straight up to that lady reporter, and slapped her across the face, hard. "How dare you question my little girl, as if she's to blame." She then took me by the arm, "Let's go home!

You'll never return to this school." Speaking directly to Mr. Button and the MP, "We will sue your asses off."

Six months in court, we won the suit filed against the school. That was twenty years ago. I went on to become an English teacher and I am proud to have succeeded in doing what I like best: teaching children and young adults to believe in themselves, and that it's never too late to change for the better.

Never let anyone or anything bring you down.

Stand Tall!

Stand up for your rights, and always be prepared for anything; keeping in mind that the grass is really greener on the other side.

Kindness

Mary Francisco

There she was, this miniature poodle, trapped in the neighbours' fence. I went to her aid. Carefully, I guided her out. "See that you don't get into that again," I told her. Then I went on my way.

The next day, that little dog followed me everywhere. I would brush her off and ignore her. I rode my bike to school and I would see her, she would tag along. I would yell at her, "LEAVE ME ALONE!" She would stop in her tracks and whimper. I'd look back and see that she had the biggest, saddest eyes, but I didn't care. I had no time for her. I knew she was a stray and I wanted nothing to do with her. But she was always there waiting, waiting, and waiting. For three weeks.

As soon as she would see me, her tail would go back and forth and she'd follow me 'til I reached home. She wanted to play. "Get out of here!" I would yell at her, but she wouldn't move. I'd look out from my kitchen window and there she'd be. ALWAYS! "Go away," I would shout at her. She would sit there – three, maybe four hours, then she'd walk away with her tail between her legs. And every time she left, I'd say, "Good, go away and don't come back."

One day, as I went to school, she was nowhere in sight. "YES! Finally, she's gone." The next day, I didn't see her again, then the next and the next. It was five days later and I started wondering, "Where is that dog?" After not seeing that dog for a week, I actually started missing her. "Where is she? Maybe something happened to her."

I went out looking for her after school for three or four days. I finally found her behind a deserted apartment building with overgrown weeds and bushes. I went to her and she looked at me with those sad eyes and whimpered, then looked away. I moved closer – then stopped in my tracks. I understood – there she was with her babies.

She looked very weak. Not only did she have her pups, but she was also wounded. Something had happened to her. My heart went out to her, and that's when I decided to take her home; her and her babies. That was five years ago today. I did keep one of her babies and sold the rest.

One month ago, she and I went for a hike. That day, I decided to go through another trail. Although she barked at me when I went down that trail, I paid her no mind. I wasn't far into the trail when the earth beneath me gave way. Down I went with the earth, but luckily I was at the edge. She tried to help me, but I was stuck. My leg was trapped beneath some wood. My little dog ran to get help and help she brought. Two men came to my aid. If it wasn't for her, maybe the earth would've swallowed me up. That's why I'd like a "dog of honour" award.

She deserves it – my little dog, Kindness.

Beast

Roberta Taylor

Sniff, I shuffle and notice
He smells too sweet
Perfume on an angry man
Can't breathe
        such
            an aroma

Get me away
Let me crawl through
            mud and heavy rain
Let me be natural
            like a beast
or
        beautiful
            wild
                creature
Standing at
            the edge
   of summer and winter
   praying to the moon
   howling at the sky
            I
am a little beast
waiting till tomorrow
        to live out loud
            or jump into
        the dark lake.

Bedmates

Rana Khan

He remembered vividly the night he had first found a sheep in his bed. He had gone to bed slightly earlier than usual that evening, and found himself awake in the middle of the night. He had turned over to seek out Jean, but there was no Jean. Instead, a sheep was sleeping quietly; head on the pillow and its soft fleece generating a warmth that probably had led him to seek out its source.

Funnily enough, he was not as alarmed as one would expect. The sheep was so non-threatening, its warmth so reassuring that he didn't jump out of the bed in fright. Instead, after the initial shock, he had relaxed and even put his hand out to stroke the soft belly. He did wonder about Jean — was this her new persona, or had she finally decided to absent herself from the marital bed? After forty odd years of marriage, he had become accustomed not only to her face but her unspoken messages, and it seemed to him that she had signaled just then that the sheep was right to be where it was. So after patting the fleecy creature, he had fallen asleep again, waking up to the usual aroma of coffee and pancakes. Jean always made pancakes on Saturdays, and there she was, in her patterned dressing gown and inscrutable face, setting the breakfast table as she did every morning.

He didn't mention the sheep at all. He thought Jean might say something about it, but she didn't, so he just ate his pancakes (with plenty of the home-churned butter, strawberry jam and maple syrup) and then went outside to the vegetable patch to check on the tomatoes. He believed in letting things be, and had tended to their farm with that philosophy for more than four decades now, after Jean had inherited it at her widowed father's death. If Jean could continue making pancakes like she did and generally make life easy for him, why should he worry about something that might have been just his imagination? So when night time came, he had quite forgotten about the sheep in his bed. He had patted Jean as usual, turned over and fallen asleep. But sometime in the night he had woken up again, conscious of a smell, and had turned over to prod Jean awake, only to see a billy goat, the angular planes of its head and beard and neck clearly outlined on the pillow. The smell was much stronger now, and he quickly turned his back on its source. What was happening to Jean — first a sheep, and now a billy goat! Couldn't a man just sleep peaceably in his bed after a hard day's work?

Yet in the clear light of the day, and after an especially fine breakfast of eggs, bacon, toast and a good helping of sweet potato fries, the memory of the billy goat faded away. Jean was her usual impassive self, not encouraging much talk at the breakfast table beyond what chores needed to be done. The message he got was that all was fine, so he didn't bother to remark upon her nightly disappearance, but instead, went out to make himself useful. That had been pretty much the pattern since he had been presumptuous enough to propose marriage to the boss's daughter, and, much to his surprise, had been accepted — a man with no family, just a steadfast worker who liked farming and his food.

That night he even had a sense of anticipation of what or whom he might find in his bed, but he'd slept soundly so presumably whatever nonsense Jean was up to had stopped.

However, the next week it had happened again, and this time there was a cow — no wonder he had been pushed almost to the edge of the bed, and his first reaction was relief at not having fallen down. He thought he recognized Bella, and it was natural that with her teats just close by, he would reach over and then suck at them. The milk tasted wonderful and refreshing (he had been thirsty, he realized) and he felt a warmth in his body that he hadn't felt for a long, long time. He had actually looked at Jean with wonder the next morning, but, as usual, she wasn't giving anything away. The oatmeal was superb, though as it always was, and with the fresh fruits alongside, he had to admit that Jean made a mean breakfast for sure. He did wish though that she had put in some sausages on the side, but then thought of the ham sandwiches she had packed for lunch along with the frozen ice tea that he liked, and so happily went off to check the cucumbers.

He let Jean pretty much alone as far as the running of the farm was concerned, especially as she was so good at it. After all, there was money in the bank, and they were debt-free when so many of their fellow farmers were in trouble with their loans. Throw in Jean's fine meals and the comfort of a good bed and he was content, even with the recent happenings at night.

So it was not much of a surprise to find rabbits and dogs and hens — even a deer — sharing his bed; though he'd draw the line at snakes and skunks. He thought he must have indicated as much to Jean, in that silent communication they had shared since their marriage, because even though there were geese and turkeys; and even that young foal and then its mother — a fine mare — in his bed, there were no unpleasant surprises.

However, if he had asked Jean about his unusual bed-mates, she would not have been surprised about them. After all, she'd been sleeping next to a pig for more than forty years herself.

Family – The F Word

Christina Walsh

Whenever I hear the word "family" mentioned, I want to say f— off or die (F.O.O.D for short). I hate my family, all of them, for what they did to me, what they denied me, and who they are. How they neglected me on purpose, how they seemed, more than anything, to be just cruel, withholding cheap-skates. I'm ashamed of them, and so I'm also ashamed of "where I come from". The word family immediately conjures up all kinds of negative, painful, lonely experiences for me. I feel like a time bomb is ticking inside of me, ready to go off on those who ask: "Do you have family here?" "Where are your family?" "Are you close to your family?" My answers, in order, are: "No." "I don't know or care." and, "No, I am not!!"

If the paragraph above offends you, I'm sorry. I am not trying to offend anyone. But if it shocks you, good. Because sometimes people need to be shocked to recognize a reality they can't see. The fact is, not everyone has a loving, supportive family. I didn't from the time I was 2 years old. And I'm not alone. John Bradshaw, creator of the PBS series 'Bradshaw on the Family', wrote that 96% of all families are "to some degree dysfunctional, that is, the system by which the family interacts is distorted by the addictions and compulsions of one or more members, and so ignores the needs of each individual." In my family, I was usually that individual. And if you can believe John Bradshaw, I'm not alone. There's a large cohort of us in the world, and, I think I can speak for them in conveying to you what we feel about this topic.

Number One: we hate hearing about other people's happy, close-knit family experiences. These descriptions choke us inside, they poison us, they make us bitter. And we don't want to be bitter. We don't want to be isolated, then kicked while we're already down exactly because we don't have anyone to call "family". Yet we're consistently kicked when we're down in this way, and, worse, silenced by people when we try to describe our own experiences.

I'm not saying that the people who do this are being malicious. They're just ignorant. Here's what I, and countless people like me, hear all the time; "I don't know what to say." and; "I can't imagine not having a loving family." Comments like this seem to be sympathetic, but in fact they're the opposite of real empathy or compassion. Here is what true empathy and compassion sound like: "Is there anything I can do to make you feel better?", "How can I include you in my life?", "What would including you in my life look like for you?" Or simply, "I'm here for you." People like me almost never near this. Instead we get comments of commiseration, comments that say; "We're sorry for you." and, "That's terrible." These comments aren't helpful, because they ignore the sharpest ache we suffer: the ache of shame.

This is the message Number Two from us to you out there. Not having what you take for granted makes us feel stigmatized, like scapegoats; we feel less than people. Not only are we unloved, but we're often unloving, because we never learned any other way. If you lack empathy and compassion in dealing with us, we lack it in dealing with others, and we know we lack it, which makes us feel even smaller and more flawed. In the end it feels as though we're considered diseased for not having loving, supportive, warm families. From where we stand, we're shunned, blamed for our lot in life, and emotionally isolated because of it. To be diseased for us is to be "dis-eased". We are without ease or peace, at a loss, unsettled, empty, and always, it feels to us, alone. All of this adds up to one simple, sharp result: it hurts.

So here it is the Final Message to you from all of us, for whom the world “family” means something very different from what it means for you. If you found yourself chatting with a group of people that included some people who had lost their legs, you probably would avoid talking about the great joys of running and jumping. So the next time you’re talking to a group of people that includes some people you don’t know, and you get an itch to brag about your wonderful, perfect families, think about the invisible wounds some of the strangers around you might be living with.

Then change the subject. Please.

Deacon Chance

Colin Buchanan

Highway One parallels the Mississippi River as it snakes its way through the Delta. Stringtown, Beulah, Waxhaw are some of the vast metropolises to be found. I had been driving for hours and grown weary of looking at just the cotton fields – though they are beautiful in bloom, snow-caps atop the jungle green as the bolls take over, kudzu swallowing what trees and shacks that remained standing. It's the hottest heat you ever felt. 100 degrees, 90% humidity, and it's so flat it feels like the sun is about a hundred feet off the ground.

I had 4-60 air conditioning: 4 windows, 60 miles an hour. I was swimming in sweat. So around about Lobdell I decided to cut over on Gulley Loop Road and ride for a while on the levee. There are at least small forests standing watch over the river behind, a few cows to look at, and the red clay of the levee road leaves whorls flying behind a car that validate the feeling of being in absolute Hell.

I was cruising along spewing pebbles and clay for a good bit, Sonny Boy Williamson loud on the tape deck, knowing I had a long drive ahead and enjoying the lack of traffic until I hit Memphis, or, anyway, until I hit the casinos in Tunica County. Feeling all right, though my destination wasn't going to be a picnic.

Then I noticed the temperature gauge on the car screech way over into the red, in the same instant huge white puffs of smoke came pouring out from under the Subaru's hood. I stop and shut the engine, flip the hood switch and the trunk switch. I'd been driving bad cars in the Delta long enough to know to always keep a jug or two of water in the trunk. Opening the hood all the way, I jumped back as a giant billow of smoke pours out. When the smoke mostly cleared out, I poured as much of the jug as I could over where it seemed the smoke was coming from. Smoke changed to steam. It was Hell. I stood back and watched until it stopped, panting, sweating.

*

It came to pass that a big red pickup came chugging slowly along. Young guy, who I'd later find out was Effie, unfolds from the cab. Turns out his daddy has a garage just up the road in Rosedale, and his truck wouldn't have a problem towing my little car. He didn't speak much, just kept muttering "Head gasket, head gasket material that white smoke is, man, head gasket." I don't know much about cars but know that a head gasket costs a whole lot more money to replace than I had. Turned out Effie was wrong.

We came crashing down off the levee road and around a winding, slow-banked curve into the south part of Rosedale. A white, cinder block building that was painted frightfully bright but seemed to be completely black on the inside. Big Amoco sign that said, "Chance Garage: We Fix Flat Tires." More than that.

I walk in and it's even hotter inside. Effie had just left my car sitting outside in the dusty parking lot. An old man, the colour that they used to call "high-yellow," wearing a baseball cap that looked 40 years old nods at me and says nothing as he walks out to the car as Effie keeps saying "head gasket." Effie had his heart set on the head gasket. Effie was all-in for the head gasket. The old man peers in for what may have been a minute, didn't touch anything, but had Effie move something toward the back for him.

"It's your pre-heater hose, boss," he tells me when he comes back, starts mopping his brow and chest with a nasty towel. "Don't cost much, don't take long to fix, but Effie's gonna have to ride over to Cleveland to pick it up for us, hear? You in a hurry?" He let out a soft gentle near-giggle. "Hope not."

*

So it came to pass that Effie lit out for Cleveland and the old man told me to come on out to the back. When I turned the corner and looked at the back window, I saw painted in stylized, incongruously elegant script; "Filling Station Church Of Christ."

"Come on in, got some air blowing in here."

There was an ancient Coca Cola ice chest in the corner, equally ancient tools against the walls, looked like they were part of the walls, dark and seemed somehow foggy. It wasn't quite a dirt floor but there was so much dirt it may have well been. I asked him if he was the Pastor of the Filling Station Church Of Christ.

"Nah-sir. That's my cousin's – he's the Pastor. I'm a Deacon." He gestured to a metal seat. The air conditioning felt so good I'd have sat on spikes.

Deacon Chance brought me a 40 oz. malt liquor. Set down on the 2x10 pew, popped his beer, grinned as a judge might, raised his bottle in toast.

"So that hose and labour," Deacon Chance paused a little and rubbed the back of his neck, "that's gonna run you I'd say 50 dollars. That gonna work?"

"Yes sir," I said. "Effie was saying it was a head gasket and ..."

"Awww," Deacon Chance cut me off. "Effie trying to learn, and when a head gasket do blow it sends out white smoke like your little car done... but ain't nothing but a hose.

You blow that head gasket on that little car of yours with all them miles on it you just leave it settin' by the side of the road, hear?"

"Yes sir," I said again. I wasn't from the Delta and didn't always follow the rules; like, I was a white man saying "yes sir" to a black man. But he was old, he was going to fix my car for me, and for Chrissake, he was a Deacon.

"This hose gonna get me to Chicago?" I asked Deacon Chance. I wasn't headed for Chicago but figured Deacon Chance would have no idea of where I was actually headed, so Chicago seemed about equivalent.

"Getchoo anywhere you want to go."

Despite the unplanned rest stop, I felt calmer than I'd felt in a long time. It was quiet except for the whirr of the AC and what sounded like a bit of catarrh from Deacon Chance as he puffed on his Newport.

Deacon Chance leaned forward towards me a bit. "You're not a religious man, are ya?"

"No sir."

"But you is a speerchal man, ain't ya?"

"Yes sir."

Cackle. Raised bottle.

"I knowed it, son, soon's I saw Effie haulin' yer car in, I said 'now that is a speerchal man.' I was right, right?"

"Yes sir. I knew as soon as I laid eyes on you, too, that you are a righteous man. I knew I was cool, all was safe." I meant it.

"You can b'lee dat, son." I very much appreciated Deacon Chance calling me "son."

Deacon Chance stood up, tripped a little in his unlaced boots, and walked over to the oil barrel, which served as the pulpit for the Filling Station Church Of Christ. He pulled a candle – Be Gone Evil – from a box behind the pulpit and lit it, then lit a Newport from the wick and set the Be Gone Evil candle upon the pulpit. He trundled back down to the pew.

"It's a new day brother," said Deacon Chance as he raised his bottle and clicked mine.

"Yes sir, it is. I could really use a new damn day."

"You gotchoo yer new damn day, brother, hear? Whatchoo wantin' to do with yer new damn day, brother?"

"Go see someone," I hadn't said this out loud yet, "I've been needing to see for a long damn time."

"All right! Does this person need to see you, too? Maybe for a long time, too?"

"Yes sir. I believe so." I believed so.

"Now son, don'tchoo believe everything you think, hear?" Another Deacon Chance chuckle followed by a coughing fit.

"Or I hope so." I hoped so. "Maybe I know so." I wasn't sure if I knew. "Even if she doesn't know so. You know what I think I'm gettin' at here, sir?"

"Ooo, brother, I mean! I remember one time going to see somebody I really needed to see, hear? And she's sittin' in that blue house over yonder right now, hear? An' son," big cackle, "thirty five years on she's still making my blood boil, hear?"

"Yes sir, I heard that."

"You can find you a blood-boiler, son, you ain't got nuttin' to fear! Not in this world and damn sure not in the next."

I didn't have the heart to tell Deacon Chance I was going to see my sister who was lying in a hospital bed with 56 stitches in her left arm. She had cut herself up in a large way, taken a load of pills washed down with a fifth of vodka. She was really trying. Got lucky her fuckwit ex-boyfriend had dropped by to retrieve his jacket which he thought made him look like a biker – it didn't; he was a periwinkle and everyone who saw him or spoke to him knew it.

I didn't acknowledge yet that she wasn't who I was really going to see. The "rescue" of my sister was an unwitting subterfuge to try to stumble upon the person who, 25 years earlier, and through not a whit of fault of her own, had left me emotionally paralyzed to this day. If I could make my sister feel better, and make myself feel anything, anything at all, the trip would be a success.

Connection

Nikhil Rajasekharan

She might have dozed off, or was she simply day-dreaming? Her waking life was a nightmare.

She had a sense of urgency due to her sudden anxiety and nervousness towards the tasks she had at her hands. She moved towards her in-house library which was lined with exquisite book racks. The library resembled a tree-house.

She was taken aback by a feeling she was getting from the sensory of her mind. A thick fog descended and she became aware of a state of fearfulness threatening to take over her physical and mental state. She instinctively kept her hand on her chest, and began rubbing the area tentatively in hopes of clearing the fog, her palms and fingertips her only defense. But it just worsened the fear and the pain. Her brain went into overdrive with a feeling of despair that she had not felt before.

She instantly longed for someone, anyone, to hold her. Someone to hug and console her, to reassure her that everything would be fine. She felt as if she was hanging from the top of the mighty CN tower with complete fear and pandemonium painted on her face.

A phone call jolted her back to reality. "Who could this be, and why is some unknown stranger calling, me?" She heard her voice shaking, shivering and trembling when she finally answered the call after what seemed an eternity. An international number flashed on her screen and the sweet voice she heard reflected compassion and empathy, the beautiful accent brought serenity to her mind.

Aurora was her name, and she said she had important news for Heather Jones. And Heather Jones became aware Aurora was indeed screaming from the other side, something about an accident and asking her to confirm if she was indeed Heather Jones.

Heather hurriedly dressed and ran as fast as she could on her nimble feet and hailed the first taxi in her vicinity. Jumping into the back seat, she just said, “Airport.” A retrospective wave hit her from the bottom of her stressed mind as she slumped into the seat.

Heather could see herself in front of her dresser mirror, almost instantly as she closed her eyes, in the backseat of that taxi. Standing 5’2”, her cute, slender body and baby face, she was wearing an oversized V-neck and long-flowing skirt, its intricate designs in green and brown, resembling plants under a blue sky. She had a nose ring her mom had gifted to her on her 18th birthday.

*

Heather looked into Aurora’s olive-green eyes with a tearful face and struggled to keep herself together. Aurora sensed Heather’s body flinch, posing a silent question of “What’s happening” and “Why is this happening to ‘ME’?” Aurora was calm and composed which surprised Heather in a way that she could not understand. One look from Aurora made Heather attentive, just enough to hear all about the tragic mystery that had recently unraveled, the mystery that had caused Aurora to fly all the way from Helsinki to Toronto.

*

Armed with her new Nikon d750+28mm f/1.8 handheld camera, a perfect machine made to absorb the beauty of landscapes, Aurora stepped onto the pavement. People yelling around her broke her concentration. She tripped as she turned and fell with her finger jammed on the clicker. As she held onto her dear camera, it kept clicking and flashing continuously at the scene developing in front of her.

The rented car skid on the pavement before it hit the bridge railing with a strong force. The railing just about absorbed the force, causing it to buckle and a sliver of metal was all that remained. Aurora, startled for a moment, snapped out and yelled "112" running towards the car. She peered over the car-window ledge, right through the shattered glass. She brushed off the glass shards and opened the door.

She dragged a middle-aged man out of the tangled mess. The man half-moaned and groaned while putting up resistance when Aurora touched him. There was concern, pain and shock in his eyes as he tilted his head looking to check-up on the lady (probably his wife) who was on the adjacent seat. The middle-aged lady was staring elsewhere with blood dripping from her face. Aurora sighed at the sight, with a silent nod towards the man. He let go of his resistance as she sat down in a bid to let him lie on her lap. The man struggled to breathe; yet somehow managed to give Aurora, a name and a number, while still looking deep into her eyes. She saw hope and faith in his eyes outlined with shocked pain. Aurora was still on the border of shock and reality herself when she gazed deep into his brown eyes. She stealthily pocketed his wallet as paramedics whisked him away. As soon as she finished answering what she needed to answer, she was on the move to the Airport placing a call to a Toronto number, the number of a Heather Jones.

That phone call affected Heather in a way she did not comprehend. Her mind became frenzied and she suddenly heard herself laughing. Her high-pitched laughing turned into a crazy, loud mouthed whimper, to uncontrollable sobs and a loud-pitched cry.

Heather was wide awake when Aurora called a second time and asked her to come to the airport café. Her brain sized up the chubby Finnish girl sitting down across from her. For a moment she got lost in Aurora's beautiful expressive olive eyes. Standing at 5'4, with an oval face, Aurora wore a black V-neck with golden prints of a beehive and a bee on a flower; the caption read, "Save Bees, Save Nature". Her shoulder-length brunette hair highlighted her dimples when she smiled. Around her neck she wore a golden feather-pendant, complimenting her perfect skin tone.

As soon as they greeted each other, Heather got a view of the whole accident unraveling, Aurora filled in the missing pieces. "You know Heather, you have your father's eyes," she said. Being around her psychiatrist parents, Aurora had learned about mental disorders, especially depression. "You know, you can talk to me about anything. I would love to help you deal with your grief." Aurora had sensed a storm brewing in Heather, but had not gauged the ferocity. Heather exploded, "Why do you care?" pausing a moment as if expecting the words to sting. Aurora recoiled, but smiled right back at her; a wide smile showing the beauty of her dimples and her expressive eyes. Aurora had a loving look on her face, which prodded Heather to open up. Heather was a recovering drug-addict who had severed ties with everyone she knew, something they call a "door-slam" and now, when she needed someone, no one was with her. This had caused depression to seep into her mind and soul. "How do I help this beautiful baby-faced girl sitting right in front of me?" Aurora thought.

She gave Heather time to come to terms with the immediate situation while she placed a call to Aaron, one of her other friends, asking him to come to the airport café ASAP. Aaron arrived and turned to the ladies, saying, "Let's go." Heather looked at Aurora and Aaron quizzically while following them instinctively.

*

An ornate, wrought iron gate with intricate designs adorned the neighborhood they were about to enter. Two unicorns on their hoofs with a beautiful rainbow connecting the horns ushered them in, giving Heather a warm feeling which broke the shackles of the chain that been wound around half of her mind. The building was rustic, but the chic interior was the most beautiful architecture she had ever seen. This place oozed a sense of belongingness. People were going about their own business without judging others. Her mind whispered to her, “This is the place you need for a fresh start”, and Heather nodded at her powerful instinct.

She felt happiness filling places of mind she never knew existed. The sights engraved into her memory. A sudden excitement engulfed her from within. She felt like a sculptor building a sculpture from inside, removing all her unnecessary fears. She understood the true value of trusting her instincts and, armed with a new determination, Heather thanked Aurora. And Aurora smiled.

A Cross To Bear – Chapter One:

Saneesha Sammy

Freezing. The air was freezing as he saw his own breath escape his lips. He couldn't see where he was or what he was doing, but somehow, his body didn't feel like his. Closing his eyes tightly, he then reopened them, hoping to have woken up but instead, could only make out the sound of a muffled voice screaming out into the distance. He tried to move his feet, but they wouldn't budge. Suddenly, the voice was right beside him. It cried out again, only this time it wasn't muffled by the distance.

He was holding something. Something soft. A napkin? No. A cloth? "Maybe," he thought, moving it around in his hand. It was damp. There was something on it, but he couldn't tell what. Something moved against him. He jumped, startled. He began to panic, feeling the cold beads of sweat formulate atop his skin.

Just then something fell to the ground. He hadn't noticed he'd been holding anything else. Was it... moving? "Oh god..." he thought once he began to make out the shape. "Oh god no..." he backed away. "No..."

"NO!"

Drenched in sweat, Daniel sat up in bed, wide awake and gasping for air. The nightmare again. Four nights in the past week the blurry set of images had come to him while he slept, vanishing into thin air as soon as he woke up. All he could ever seem to recall were shadowy figures, muffled sounds, and the panic in his own voice saying, "No!"

Daniel glanced down at Emily beside him. She was still asleep. He figured that she had just grown accustomed to what he jokingly referred to as his "Twilight Zone Terrors" during the earliest days of their relationship. At least enough to be able to sleep through them more often than not. Back then, they were sporadic and out of the blue. In the last three months, however, they had become increasingly more frequent, leaving barely a trace of their existence in Daniel's memory at all. Unlike regular nightmares, which he'd always chalked down to as being a part of the job seeing what he saw and knowing what he knew, at least he could recall them upon waking up. The other kind of nightmares, like the one he had tonight, were in a different category all of their own. One moment they were here, and then, like smoke, they were gone.

Emily shifted in her sleep. He slid back down between the sheets and curled his arm around her. She pulled him in closer. The warmth of her body was his saving grace. He knew better than to keep secrets from her, and yet, he couldn't bring himself to tell her the truth about how bad the dreams had gotten. If she hadn't already figured it out, it wouldn't be long before she did. After all, putting the pieces together was kind of in her job description.

Emily, now his fiancée, didn't always used to be. She was working as a psychologist at the precinct dealing with first responders before she had been assigned to him by his commanding officer three and a half years ago. The premise of their sessions began as a mandatory follow-up to his partner of five years being shot and killed on the job. Only after a few months of therapy did Emily theorize that Daniel's nightmares weren't the result of the homicide, but rather that the homicide had just caused them to resurface. Daniel rejected the idea. Instead, he would tell her that his nightmares were nothing more than an occupational hazard. As long as any cop in the Murder Squad carried a precinct badge, their everyday realities would be far worse than any of the nightmares that always seemed to follow. For the most part, he thought he'd convinced her.

And now this.

"Daniel?"

She wasn't asleep. At least not anymore. "Another one?" The question was rhetorical.

"It's fine, go back to sleep," he said.

She rolled over and placed her head on his chest. He knew exactly why she did this. It was to listen to the pace of his heartbeat that – unlike him – would always tell the truth. "You're a terrible liar."

"Maybe."

"If you're having them again, just talk to me. I'm not blind, you know."

"I know."

"Then why won't you talk to me? You do remember what I do for a living, don't you?"

He didn't answer.

"Something's going on up there Danny," she tapped her index finger against his temple. "I wish you'd just talk to me instead of keeping everything bottled up."

He kissed her forehead, smelling the shampoo she liked to use. "It's probably just work. You know how stressful it can be at the precinct, and this case," he paused, "it's just a tough one, that's all."

"They're always tough Danny, but you don't always wind up with the nightmares." She had a point. He knew she had a point. "You're holding something down and until you either figure out what it is or let someone help you, then it's just going to keep holding you down with it." She paused. "Maybe we should call Mary—"

"Forget it, Em. I told you, there's no way I'm going to let

Marie-Anne hypnotize me. It's just a load of bullshit."

"And how would you know? You've never gone through with it. What if she might actually be able to help you?"

"Listen, I'll figure it out on my own, and if I can't, then you can call Marie-Anne LeClair. Deal?"

"Fine," she said. "Deal." Daniel had always been impressed by her ability to hold back the frustration in her voice when it came down to difficult topics. He knew it was most likely a side effect to her profession, but it was one that he admired. "But promise me that if you can't get a handle on it, you'll let me make the call," she said, punching his shoulder.

"Ow, that hurt," he smiled back at her.

"Promise me Daniel."

"I promise." She shifted upwards against the sheets to nuzzle her face between his neck and collarbone.

"Good."

"But I know I'll sort it out myself. I guarantee it."

*

The following morning, sitting behind the wheel of his black Toyota Corolla heading straight towards the downtown core, he wasn't so sure. The fact that it was the coldest day of winter thus far certainly didn't help. He wasn't sure how it could even be possible for the temperature to drop below zero Fahrenheit in New York City without hell itself freezing over, but somehow, there he was, sitting in an icebox and listening to the weather man tell him that today's low was going to feel like -1 with the wind chill. It was just the cherry on top of an already fantastic 24 hours, he thought to himself, peering through the vapor encircling the Tri-City Bridge.

The station's parking lot was filled with the same cars in

the same exact locations they had always been in as far back as Daniel could recall. He hit reverse and slid the Corolla between a white Chevy Pickup and a navy blue Toyota – Charlie's and Frank's. As he shut the door behind him, he compared the Pickup to his own. Though he would never admit it, he didn't quite mind the compromise to a more suburban car if it made Em happy. That was all that really mattered, and if she was happy, so was he. Daniel left both cars behind as he made his way towards the station.

Frank was standing behind the front desk and by the change in his expression the moment Daniel walked in, he knew something was wrong.

"Dan, Cormack's been looking for you. We've got another dead girl, same MO as the last."

"Shit." He wasn't expecting another one so soon. "When?" He asked, quickening his pace.

"About 20 minutes ago. A guy found her in a cemetery up north, said she was covered with branches and wrapped in a garbage bag. Forensics are on the scene now. They say she's about 21, but they're still working on an ID." Frank came to a complete stop in the middle of the hallway, forcing Daniel to do the same. He turned to face him and by the look on Frank's face, he knew there was something else and that he wasn't going to like it. "She had nothing on her but a cross Danny..."

Before Frank could finish, Daniel's jaw clenched as he felt the pressure of his anger inside his temples. "I swear to God, I'm going to catch this fucker if it's the last thing I do."

Frank paused. "I believe you."

"There you are, Rhodes," Daniel and Frank turned to see Chief William Cormack speeding towards them with a case file in one hand and a set of keys in the other.

"Sir," both greeted as the chief motioned for them to follow.

"I assume your partner's filled you in?" the chief said, maintaining his pace.

Daniel nodded. "So she was found in a graveyard?"

"Apparently. I'm headed there now, we'll take my car."

Daniel hesitated, and looked at Frank. "Sir, are we sure it's the same unsub?"

There was a brief moment of silence, "Yes."

"It's just that," Daniel continued, "our unsub is usually a lot more careful in where he places his victims, more discreet. This just seems a little too... uncharacteristic. Almost as if—"

"He wanted her found," said Frank.

*

The cemetery's path was icy and layered in snow. Daniel took each step one at a time, trying not to let on that he was absolutely terrified of the clear sheets that lay beneath his feet, though he couldn't seem to place the feeling why. Cormack suddenly stopped a few feet off the trail causing Daniel to nearly walk right into him had it not been for Frank holding him back. He turned his head and briefly motioned his thanks before turning back around to face the girl in the bag lying inches deep within the snow.

The same rush of anger from earlier that morning came back for round two. Walking around the chief who was still on the phone, he headed straight towards the body as the anger distracted him from the ice that seemed to be consuming a vaster area of space the further off the trail he went. Daniel dropped to his knees once he had reached the body and noted instantly what Frank had told him prior to leaving the station. There in her hands – that were placed perfectly together in the center of her chest – was a cross.

"Danny, you ok?" Frank's voice broke the silence as he too bent down to see for himself. Immediately, they looked back at each other. The cross. It was inverted.

"Get me forensics." Daniel heard himself say. "Now!"

Trapped In A Jaded Psychosis

Rashma Manjra

A Hank without a Karen,
Reformatted in dissolution,
We disassociate to predestined assumptions
And everyone is stuck in a sad story...
So many sad stories.

A mask, maybe 2, like a personality crisis.
How long until you adversely become that contrived
persona?
Do you only know what you know just to perpetuate
that which you chase?
Man be looking hella confusing.
Outside looking in at what fucking breed this is.
Smashy smash smash your face right in and gaslight ya self
ya twat.

Should we even wake up?
Or keep speaking over our faded sad stories like it's
a competition.
Quest for some kind of pseudo logic, but I'd like to forget
people like you.
The stars remind me that there could be something new.
But nah there are just too many shape shifting users like you.
Where do y'all come from?
Is there a handbook?

Another fuck,
Another heart dead,

Get out.
We are all empty now anyway.

Are we humans born with feelings and so desperately
seeking to be heard like attention whores?
Or did we just learn that we should have feelings?
Can we just stay jaded? Jaded ain't such a bad thing.
Got my heart in a lock,
And my dreams on point.
I got myself right where I want to be.
Now to reverse the damage on my brain cell count so I can
spit fire like I was meant to.
Forget you!

Yea, we looked pretty dope together, danced until we saw
the sunrise together, but forget you. I wanted to spend
my whole life with you. Now you are finally pretending
to be here and it's too late. I am the poster child of jaded
and faded.

Everyone is walking around completely confused and
Nowadays it's ontadanext, ontadanext, call the disposal unit,
ontadanext.
Everyone is everyone's and animals watching animals.
Pressure to find deeper relevance in the wake but who
is awake?
Hello?!
If you are, then holla at me.
I'd like to stay up late with you, talk about life with you, lay
in bass waves with you. Whatever, it's dumb anyways,
but I've seen stranger things exist.

Humans are made to forget and nothing lasts, therefore
 it makes ample amount of sense to seek
 what is pragmatic.
Swallow the loneliness.
Shove it deep into the stomach and let it become the anger
 that drives you to do better than the sad sack of stories
 others throw on you.
Monkey business.
Surround yourself with all that your grind can bring you
And cry yourself to sleep every night.
That sadness will run so deep man.
It's dissociation conceptualized.
Too much
Too much for the mind to handle,
Body shock.
What's next?
Binge, purge, repeat.
Fuck until the pain runs deep,
Until you contemplate suicide because the loneliness
 is indefinable and change is deemed impossible like
 the dawn of a haze.
Chaos is a natural state,
Second nature,
Survival.
Why do I keep going to places of dehumanization?
How do I keep ending up here?
Even if I know why I still keep going because the madness
 is limitless.

Did we all deserve more at some point?
How did we get so twisted? We just do it all over again

until we are dead.
It's an approved system of the pragmatic life game.

Love is a delusion
We are created to procreate pain.
I told you until I die I'd be here.
Well the heart is fickle.
Now dip.
Got my Henny.
Got a line of D.
What more do I need?
Out.

(But wake up.
This might be a subconscious persona.
A survival tactic to stop the pain from seeping in.
Through psychedelic ego deaths I give life a second shot.
I feel different
A little less jaded.
This is a reminder that I'm not fully dead).

The Fentanyl Release

p.a.eng

Snore God snore. Make some noise. Peddle me a dream. Surf me away with your power and glory. Embrace my scream of courage. I am drowsy for love. Tell me something warm or cast me away like a nickel of shame. The sky is wet with townsfolk chatter. Forget me not Wednesday or Ash General Day or any day homogenous hometown and typical. Obtain for me that slender time. Extinguish my sorrow under your blue cast sky. Ply me from this doublethink gimmickry world enchanted with painted sunsets and check out girls with pink rouged faces and long brown hair in stores that give away cravings and flaunt your worth in the speck of a mirror. Doff a hat for me. Doff it high in the air and let it sail over the tumble moody exercise of earth and fly the randomness of your windy spectacle upon my solace. Never let me slouch and save me on this unkind day where people shout and push to get their way. Take me for a ride on this white ocean sky with sinewy clouds immaculate with brilliance, with silver linings and gold crimson smiles. Sigh to me. Make some sound. Reach me before I wake and flounder like another rag flying along the road in a shapeless mist. Am I in line to see her free and jubilant in the sun? Tell me something undrunk, unfeigned, unflagging, something possible to comprehend. Tell my flower trinket heart before I plunge off this edge of harsh occurrence and tired light. I have conquered the shores of despair to be pulled back by an undertow uncommon to me. I have been sucked back and slammed into the wet grainy sands, cut and scratched between huge bashes of unrelenting lifeless regiment waves, each as soul-less as unforgiving.

And childhood came in a delicate quiver, popping toast,

jam and butter. The dead long splendour of all her woman's glory fell off the Milky Way. She felt a spin wet cold her face. Her instant sweat. She saw the blackness and knew it was wrong.

And I said to her, "Rouse my sleepy head from your dance ball gown, oh sweetheart of my falling, I will lend a radiance to your cry and hold your hand as we step under the mute sparkle above, as we lose our course and fall to the ground beneath."

I saw the blackness and knew it was wrong.

An 'Ode' To Tamoxifin (My Cancer Medication)

Rana Khan

You came to me unbidden,
Unwanted, unsought
But doctors pronounced adjuvant therapy
and presided over a forced union.

You were unloved from the start,
Your chivalric gifts were mood swings, and brain fog
Along with a new daily ritual.
I remember the nightmare of forgetting about you, then
remembering,
The frantic call to the doctor (it was early days), when things
seemed most fragile;
But then you had just entered my life, and
I was still discovering things about you

You were possessive, I see that now, even jealous
So my insides shrank and withered, my desire absent
or fleeing
While you gloated,
And I flushed hot and cold, on and off, like a bar's neon light
blinking at night,
Long after its patrons have staggered home

Ever conniving, you even stole time, my clock biological,
The monthly ritual banished for ever
By our nightly consummation
It woke me up nights, to silently weep for what was lost
forever

So I resent you, and curse you and yet
Living with you has made it easier
For me to believe that someday
You will become more than just something swallowed,
That in fact your jealous possessiveness will destroy
    the traitor cells
That once threatened to overwhelm me,
That through my sustained loyalty to you
Will come my redemption.

Finally Defeated

Rashma Manjra

Re-structure, re-build, re-use and get used. Brain to mush. Madness becomes the primary cause of this monstrous cluster of words people utter to what they do not understand. Bass clarity twisted in life's ratchet hands. Disposability becomes the direct correlation to expect-a-bilities. Mistakes cannot become an option. Heart is deep and heavy. Possessed sanity in a delusion (perhaps) but it did feel real once. Last attempt at anything, who knows.

So elementary, level one again.

Frustration. Misunderstood.

Too fucked up inside to convey feelings.

Self-diluted psychosis.

Physically hitting bottom, the mind struggles to remain somewhat destined. Wrapped in so much confusion, weakness joins the trip.

Trigger trigger trigger bam. Shoot self in between eyes to stop the brain twist. Stop the insanity. Slut whore dumb bitch: trigger bam bam bam. No space for mistakes. Remember, no space to heal. No space to breathe and to sort out madness into little bins. Bins with tight lids

bursting,

exploding.

Product of own insanity with no stability to stand upon. Just need a chance to think, but life has no time.

Taking too much time. Making more mistakes. Clock is ticking fuck-head. Don't want to let go. Don't want to put anything away like this…

Left without words. Left without having any chance to make sense of it and told what a monster is by looking in the mirror, stripped of it all.

Just write.

One is not born with these stupid ideas in their heads. They are taught them by a society that has no place for mistakes. Egotists use love as a weapon and blast those who don't live up to its standards.

Yes, jaded. Yes, empty. So much hate in words, leaving stab wounds in chest.

Egos.

Fucked up.

Faded,

hurting.

Scared, little egos.

Relapse and drink away sadness. Bury all motivation. Relapse because that's what some want from others anyway.

Chest raw, words weak, hands sweating, tears down cheeks.

Heart sinks so deep, palpitating feelings. It's easier to choke than to find meanings in them.

Wish there was a way to understand this. To go back,
to erase actions.

Don't want some dreams to die. Never want them to die. Should learn to accept it.

Defeated.

Finally.

Who would've thought?

It will get better.

The Dream

Doug Grundman

I woke from the wet. Drenched in sweat. Looking at my arm I notice a droplet, as if my skin has bubbled from the inside. I am on my back, straight legs, arms by my side. My body, complete, touched on soft, yet sopping, wet mattress. I am neither hot nor warm. I am chilled with nothing to instinctively grab for and pull up to warm me. My sheets, heavy with this sick sopping – as if a corner of a cotton cloth was somehow dipped in a puddle and slowly the fabric absorbed that still water completely dry.

Struggling to a sitting position, shivering, my mind begins to search for calm. Think Chuck, as my body begins to cool too fast, goose bumps and cool on my skin seem separate from my thoughts. I search to understand the why, where have I been all night? What terrified or excited or spun me towards a place of anxiety of panic of fear? Eagle, I think, as I look down and see my fingers, like talons scratching my arm in tracks of subconscious anxiety. Dr. Skye's insight, not mine. I guess we'll have to consider adjusting my meds again during this week's check-in phone call. I don't need a psychiatrist to tell me my sleeps and scratches cannot continue like this much longer.

I'm alone. I always feel alone. Daylight in this room forever reminds me of the outside world that feels so distant. Sun offers me no warmth this morning, like all mornings, no solace. Only a bright light exposes, reminds me that life doesn't really feel as if it includes me.

Peeling off my top and bottom, I consider a towel to dry off, but find only dry and chatter to absorb. Dawning my sweatshirt and pants, feeling the inside fuzz welcome of fleece, I realize Roots brand is my only friend. Heavy, warm, old and comforting, softly reminds me to tread on with my routine. Walking into the kitchen I pull back the familiar curve of my wooden chair. My weight plops me down onto its hard worn seat jolting me, and I remember.

"Shit!" I scream…tense chest and stomach are put aside, my heart electric bolts …. Cockroach.

Yoga ninja grace combine, I effortlessly sweep reach for my book. With a motion that mimics the art of a martial master's wisdom, words arch as if a pendulum has gone skyward in one continuous path, rises up, rushing silently through its arc and slam – done – death.

I feel my body return. Shoulders drop, as if a voice is whispering into my ear, "pause, relax". My heart beats breathe into a damp sweat – sweat…. again sweat, but only this time I am awake, not dreaming.

I take stock of my kill site and read the cover of my weapon of convenience covering its prey: "Full Catastrophe Living" by Jon Kabat-Zinn. Six hundred pages of enough weight whose aim is to calm me, has become my salvation from the unwanted – only this time Zinn, the scholar, the psychiatrist of Zen, couldn't have known his worth. I wonder if I can somehow slam it to keep out tomorrow morning's sun.

Slumping back into my chair, drained of adrenaline, my eyes sweep around my space. The breath in my ears is lessening, allowing exhales to be drowned by an unrelenting humming fridge which forever bothers me and now reminds me that I am hungry.

Getting up I lift the book and like a flash of spark, death disappears off the table's edge. My eyes widen and I am stuck, mouth open, no sound, no air, I'm remembering slam; flush solid crush, hard table and silence.

I realize there was no permanent murder, only attempted, as my prey patiently waited. That cockroach, I muse, represented fearless, endurance, ingenuity and survival. What is this? Am I whispering empathy or passion or respect?

I wish the cockroach would have stayed. Not to die, but to be admired. Really noticed. I want to learn how to be crushed and move on. I want to learn how to be patient when covered with despair, being trapped, unable to move. Patient and then to seize the moment.

The moment. That cockroach wasn't lying there with her or his brain telling him some past or future story. There wasn't any crisis reaction. Not 'what if's', or 'why didn't I', or anger or self-pity. Only the moment. The instinctive ability to hold on to reality. The reality of the now. Wait. Maybe take inventory; pain? Broken? Bent? Maybe. Or perhaps simply deal with the challenge. To endure the weight, that oppressed feeling of not being able to move. That startle of moving and then hearing and feeling a thunder so loud, unavoidable, so overwhelming. And now reality changes. The now changes. Held without an ability to move. Frozen, but not cold. Stuck, but not held. Only a weight so formidable breath feels as if lungs are viced in a torture. Stone walls have closed enough to be, but without mercy, allowing you to not live, but only breathe.

So waiting takes on the purpose of how to cherish. The now, the shitty, lower than low and alone is the cherish. The story is the brain wishing you hurt.

Now my eyes widen. Death's escape, programmed over millennia, although involuntary, is ultimately a trained muscle. To keep the brain focused on the now. We have choices. To react or respond.

I opened the door and the smell of the building welcomed

me or warned me. I wasn't sure, too early to tell. An odour, a waft of onion or was it garlic? It smelled good, like a home memory somewhere too long ago. Feeling a bit lightheaded I head for the banister to hold me on the way to the street. A lady consumed with sweeping the carpeted stairs vigorously looks up. Instantly smiling, pauses, "Good morning, have a magical day!" I couldn't resist my reaction to break into a grin, "Thanks," is all I could muster as I passed, but felt a new warmth, as if a seven-year-old's ego finally belonged, as if, finally, I wasn't being picked last to play a game.

My descent immediately felt easier. As if the wooden banister was now an escalator, rubbered guide, pulling me towards the street's traffic and rush of noise below.

Sunlight brightened the front door's pane to such a white degree that beyond the frame was masked. Pushing down on the handle, already warmed by the day, I almost shiver with the anticipation of my next step. Leaning forward the door swings easily, the light is now forcing my eyes to slit shut but I am not blind, I am awake and today I think a dream may be coming true.

Patient 250505: Small, Charles

Jake Allderdice

Dr. Carlsbad says "Go ahead, Charles."

It's always 'Charles,' never 'Charlie' with him. Nobody else calls me Charles, except Mom and Dad—but only when they're mad. My sister sometimes calls me 'Shirley,' but that's because she couldn't say Charlie when she was little. Everyone thought her dumb lisp was cute. Except me, obviously. Now that she's 12, she mostly doesn't do it anymore, except to bug me.

But Dr. Carlsbad says Charlie's a boy's name: "You're 17. You're a man." Sure I am. Actually, I'm an actor. Give me a part to play. I'll be the man. Here's what I am: obese; sexually immature; conflicted. I spied on what Dr. Carlsbad wrote, if you want to know. He wrote: Body Dysmorphia, which I looked up: "self-perception out of kilter with a person's actual appearance." He wrote: Homosexual? Like that, with a question mark.

Can we not talk about this? It was bad, what I did. It's bad to spy. Seeing stuff you're not supposed to see only messes everything up, for everyone. But it happened. Get over it.

So anyway, I don't mind him calling me Charles. It makes me feel serious and important. Like what I have to say is important. Only I don't actually have much to say. I mean, I have a lot to say, but what I have to say, I can't say: obviously not to Dr. Carlsbad. So, I spend my week thinking of a script for myself: a part I can play… a guy who has weird dreams. .

*

Because I do have weird dreams, to be honest. When I remember them.

Dr. Carlsbad likes hearing my dreams. He says, "Write

them down; that helps." He says, "Go ahead." He says, "It's not the dream you have that matters. It's what you tell about it."

"You mean if I just make stuff up, even that's okay?"

He grins. "Of Course! Sometimes what a person claims happened is just as useful as what may actually have happened."

"How do you know the difference though?"

He just grins. So certain things about Dr. Carlsbad will make you wonder.

*

It's true I never remember them, in any case. My dreams. And when I do remember them, it's because I woke up half-way through. So, I don't know how they end. What's the good of a story without an ending?

*

What else. For one thing, he conducts his sessions with you on one chair, him on another, sitting kitty-corner to a small Gustav Stickley table, the kind with the dark oak finish and the slatted sides, the four square posts. How do I know this? So, I'm into antiques. So, I'm weird that way. My aunt says it's cool to love antiques. She says I might be an architect, like her.

But I'm not anything, okay? I'm an actor.

He's got all these antiques: a rolltop desk with a million compartments and Stickley furniture and a Seth Thomas ship's clock tick-tocking away on the shelf where he can keep an eye on it. He collects antique wind-up toys, too.

But what I'm saying is there's no hierarchy. A square table. Kitty-corner. There's no hidden doctor snoozing behind you like in the New Yorker cartoons, some old blank-eyed dude twiddling his thumbs or reading pornography while you prattle on. No leering old fart murmuring incantations or notes of encouragement. No: with Dr. Carlsbad, you face each other, like friends: pals, even. He's not even that old, actually. He's like a wiser, older brother.

Sometimes he tells you something from his own life, in fact: some small revealing detail that encourages you to believe you're not crazy after all; everybody's conflicted. You could almost forget your parents are paying him to listen to you.

Until the 50 minutes is up, that is. Then, he stops, sometimes cutting you off, sometimes mid-sentence himself: a wind-up toy that's run down its spring. Each week, he mumbles the same thing: "Well Charles, I'm afraid we've got to stop, now."

You need to be there to see this change. One moment, it's your pal, Dr. Carlsbad, telling a sorry anecdote about Chekhov, the next, it's "So, I'll see you next week, I trust."

Chekhov? Well, yes. You might think it's because I got this part in the Three Sisters, but no. Old Carlsbad just loves quoting Chekhov: 'Medicine is my wife. Literature is my mistress.' "Or: 'To Moscow, to Moscow.'" Who's crazy again? He loves all these other MDs who were writers. He loves old Bruno Bettelheim, with his fairy tales. He likes A.J. Cronin, or E.J. Cronin, or A.R. Cronin... anyway, according to Dr. Carlsbad, Cronin's this UK medical doctor who wrote these stories about a UK medical doctor. Or Oliver Sacks. You know, The Man Who Mistook His Wife for a Hat? Doctors who wrote true accounts of their wacky patients. People eat that stuff up.

I asked Dr. Carlsbad on one occasion if he thought a doctor's patients might mind having their stories made available for public consumption.

"Oh, well," he said. "I rather think not. One wouldn't use their real names, you see." That's how he put it: One wouldn't use... Not "they." You get that, right?

"In any case, one imagines the people written about would be flattered. Those not included probably feel left out. They wonder why their stories don't make the grade. Everyone wants to be thought interesting."

*

This is true, I have to admit. I want to be thought interesting. When Dr. Carlsbad says "Go ahead," I want to have the goods for him, like anyone would. Just not the real goods.

So I tell him again about being cast in the play at school: I'm playing Andrei, the fat brother in Chekhov's Three Sisters.

"Mmm-hmm. You told me," he murmurs. Scratch-scratch, goes his pen.

I tell him again about my sister, who's been bugging me because she's always perfect and everyone loves her.

"Mmm-hmmm." He murmurs. Scratch.

I tell him again about Mom and Dad, who I think are going to get a divorce.

"Mmm-hmmm." He's not writing anything. He's heard me say this stuff before. It's not interesting to him. He's just watching me. Waiting. He wants me to tell him something new. He wants the real goods. What happened last month. The things I can never tell him...

"That reminds me," I say. "I had that dream again last night."

"Which dream?"

“I always wake up halfway through. Just once I’d like to get to the end. You know, to find out what happens. This time I wrote it down, like you said to.” I show him my journal.

“Which dream,” Dr. Carlsbad repeats.

“I kicked the blankets free. I was sweating, too. Sweating, kicking, probably punching, I’m not sure. Like I’m battling a cage. But it won’t hold. It stretches, like mesh. Like panty-hose.”

“Mmm-hmm,” says Dr. Carlsbad. He’s not writing though. “What else,” he says.

“Not panty-hose, more like weeds. Water-grass. Seaweed. Something slithery that snakes around your bare legs; you kick at it but that just draws it tighter.”

“You’re underwater.”

“But you can breathe, too, right?” “So, above the water.”

“No, you’re in the water. It’s dark, you’re definitely under it, no, but breathing’s not an issue. And one more thing—you’re not fat, anymore, because of the water? It’s kind of nice, that way—you don’t mind it… It’s just the weeds, and it’s wet, and you fight them but they don’t offer you anything to fight—they give way, but you’re still held there, you’re still hemmed in.”

“Mmm-hmm,” says Dr. Carlsbad again, making a note at last. Scratch-scratch. I’m sure he’s writing about my not feeling fat.

He never brings up my fat, but he likes it when I do it myself. He acts like he doesn’t notice me being obese, but he does. He switches the Thonet bentwood rocker to this solid oak Stickley one when it’s my session; he thinks I don’t notice but I do. He’s worried I’m going to bust through the caned seat everyone else gets to sit on.

“What happens if you don’t try to fight? How do you free

yourself if fighting just makes it worse? Why not just relax and enjoy it, not feeling..."

"...Fat?" I finish for him. "Well I don't know, do I? That's when I wake up. I always wake up before the dream ends."

"Or," says Dr. Carlsbad, "You wake up because the dream has ended."

"Or I only dream I wake up. I free myself by waking up."

"Which would mean you're still dreaming?"

I fix him with a shocked look, kind of half-kidding. "So I'm dreaming I'm here?"

"Maybe ...not as ridiculous as it sounds," says Dr. Carlsbad. "But... not what I said."

Scratch-scratch.

"I don't understand."

"Well does it feel as if you're dreaming now? Did you dream you just told me a half-remembered dream?"

"Huh?"

"Sometimes a person may feel dissociated from the life they're leading, or rather, the actual things they're doing—their actions. As if it's not them, but someone they're watching. Someone else."

"So you might do something bad. You're not to blame though."

"Is that how you feel?" Dr. Carlsbad has his clipboard and pen, and is poised, waiting for my answer.

I want to be thought interesting, it's true. But I have to be careful. He waits. I realize he's not talking about my dream any more. This has nothing to do with my fighting the water-weeds, or being able to breathe underwater, or the question of how I got there in the first place, or being obese, or not being obese, or how I got free of the weeds. This is about what happened last month. What I did. He knows. But I haven't told anyone about this. I grasp my journal in both hands. How's he know about this?

"What do you mean?" I finally say.

Scratch-scratch. Dr. Carlsbad speaks over his clipboard, his pen moving on the paper.

Scratch-scratch. "Sometimes, what we don't say is truer than anything we do say," he says. He's not even writing but I still hear it. Scratch-scratch. It's the whir of a spring-operated toy, winding down. Its gears turning, a tick-tocking.

He gazes at me over his clipboard. "Is there something you haven't said? Something you want to say?" His eyes have wandered to the ship's clock on the shelf behind me.

"I…" I say.

"...Well Charles," he says. "I'm afraid we've got to stop, now." He's over at his rolltop desk, fishing through the compartments. I can actually barely hear him, because of the scratching, whirring, turning and ticking. But you can be pretty sure what he says then is "So, I'll see you again next week, I trust?"

Open A Door

Roberta Taylor

Open the door to an
empty room
and witness all that has gone on
before

The Lovers, the newborns,
the ancient ones sitting
in repose
after a feast, lingering
before the Fire, talking
quietly or dozing in
a chair.

Now watch the hurtling
history of the occupants and the
room itself – and stop.

Nothing has changed
but
the lovers have
aged and
the newborns are now
the ancient ones,
and the
phone never
rings,
and the Dust
glistens.

Contributor Biographies

J. Letchworth Allderdice teaches architectural design, acts (though not on stage), dances (when no one's looking), and makes a mean waffle. His singing voice would surprise you. He participates in Lucile Barker's weekly "Joy of Writing" workshop. In 2016 Allderdice won sixth prize in Ve'ahavta's creative writing contest.

Tracy de Boer is an emerging writer living in Toronto. She is completing her PhD in political philosophy and has received multiple awards for her research including a grant from the Canadian Social Sciences and Humanities Research Council. Her writing has been published in *Hypatia*, *Fit is a Feminist Issue*, and *The Western News*.

Stacey Bowen is a single mom, and a person with lived experience. She graduated from the Assaulted Woman and Youth Advocate Counseling program at George Brown College and works as a Front-Line Worker at Fred Victor. As a member of the Toronto Writers Collective, she has won two awards for "She Waits" and "Shelby's House" and in 2016 an honorable mention for "Suicide".

Colin Buchanan "grew up" in various towns and cities in Ontario. He spent a decade living in the American Deep South, mostly Mississippi, which informs his writing and dancing. His literary influences include Thomas Pynchon, George Saunders, and Dr. Seuss.

Brittany Chung Campbell is a twenty-something writer living in Toronto. She started her blog, *The Twenty-Something Survival Guide*, on the night of her 20th birthday and what started out as an anonymous personal online diary has turned into a public, honest, raw account of life in her twenties.

Ana Dinar came to Canada in 1961 at the age of four, receiving Canadian Citizenship in 1977. She lives in York with her awesome sister, Mary. She began creative writing at Unison Health Centre on June 25, 2015. "Writing helps me feel whole, and I've met some very interesting people."

p. a. eng's writing passion began in Grade 10, when his high school teacher Miss Sharon urged him to improve his grammar. Since then, his poetry has been published in a newspaper and in an anthology, *Scaling the Face of Reason*. Taking a weekly poetry workshop from Annie Wong in the fall of 2016 has rekindled his drive to write.

Mary Francisco came to Canada from Portugal in 1961 at the age of 3. She enjoys writing and finds it a good way to release tension. She likes to make people laugh and enjoys the company of others. Her dream is to write a novel.

Hildegard Gmeiner's professional background is in languages, international trade, broadcast journalism and intuitive awareness consulting. At age 33, life-altering contact with extraterrestrial intelligence from Boötes/Andromeda helped her heal her then poor health, and as well as raise her four, now grown children. She writes "Experiential Fiction", poetry and also stories for children.

Doug Grundman completed his York University BA major in psychology at the age of 42. There, his writing was recognized with the Eugene H. Zimmerman Award for Best Essay. Doug's love of the written word continues and is enriched by TWC participants and supporters who believe, "*everyone who writes is a writer.*" (Pat Schneider)

Erdine (Dee a) Hope is an original participant of the Toronto Writers Collective. She is also a Facilitator, single Mother, Radio Host and Programmer with Radio Regent for five years. Her experience spans twenty years working with marginalized populations — now at Sound Times Support Services as a frontline Community Worker. The Toronto Writers Collective gave her voice, in a community of writers whose support and inclusion empowers all to tell their peers unique stories; to become a writer. The truest form Freedom.

Prabha Jerrybandan identifies as Indo-Caribbean Canadian. Born in Trinidad, she immigrated to Canada in 2003. Although English is her first language, she is very much influenced by Indian tradition, as well as a mixed cultural experience both in Trinidad and Canada. Her academic research has included stories of Indo-Caribbean women.

Rana Khan was born in India. She describes herself as 'twice-migrated', having spent almost two decades in the Middle East before moving to Canada in 2008. For her, writing has been both a shield and a mirror for her many life experiences. Rana finds herself increasingly drawn to poetry.

Penelope Klees considers herself older than Christ, an English/French speaking Black Canadian born in England, who has lived in three countries and visited twenty-five. Widowed at thirty-two, she is raising two children alone. Sadly, she has known "sheltered-life", for the homeless women in Canada. STILL — a lover of life, intelligence, palter, artist, poet! Her belief? Live together in harmony — CARE! That's her mantra!!

Rashma Manjra works as a freelance video editor and is generally a creative person. She expresses herself through dance, art, film and writing. Rashma started writing poetry when she was 14. Later it progressed to short stories and screenplays. So much has happened in her life and she wants to express that in her writing.

Jose Mario Moreira de Oliveira is a web developer interested in philosophy and good stories in general. He has written many short stories and a few uncompleted novels and saw in the Write On! program an opportunity to be more organized about his writing habits.

Neha Poduval is a trained actor from Asia's Premier Film School – *The Film and Television Institute of India*. She has been a part of various theatre productions in Mumbai. Neha is also a trained Sivananda Yoga Teacher currently living in Toronto.

Nikhil Rajasekharan has a Masters in Microbiology and is into creative writing. He is presenting his first ever written work in the Toronto Writers Collective's Front Lines Anthology. Nikhil is also into music as an amateur singer apart from being a tutor in Microbiology. He was also a professor of Microbiology in a foreign college.

Ken Rosser is a creative writing workshop facilitator at Mustard Seed with the Toronto Writers Collective. Ken's short story 'Why Do I Endure' was one of the winners of the 2016 *Words from the Street Creative Writing Contest*. Ken was diagnosed with Autism Spectrum Disorder (ASD). He is currently working on his novel, *Jemmy and Pip*.

Saneesha Sammy, born May 6, 1993, is a Toronto-based fiction writer. Having spent the better part of her years to date writing poetry — some of which has already been published — she now spends her time attending writing courses, constructing fictional novels, and self-publishing pieces of them online.

Ward Smyth's urban poetry combines multisyllabic and intricate internal rhymes with vibrant storytelling, woven with life experiences and tied together by unbridled passion. Be sure to keep your eyes and ears open for his upcoming albums "*The True Ward; Strong & Free*" EP and LP.

Roberta Taylor was born in Winnipeg and spent her early childhood in foster care. After being adopted at age 7, she went to theatre school and studied classical music. She also spent time on a farm. Today, at 56, Roberta sells art and photography. Despite physical challenges, Roberta feels she is now at her most creative.

Christina Walsh has always known and believed that she is a writer. She writes authentically to inspire, help and be a voice for others. Christina believes in the power of words and self-expression. Writing gives her energy and purpose. Her go to 'trio' are pen, paper, and fingers.

The Mentors

Puneet Dutt holds a MA in English from Ryerson University. She is the author of the chapbook *PTSD south beach* (Grey Borders Books), which was a Finalist for the 2016 Breitling Chapbook Prize. Her poetry has been published in a number of journals and in *Imaginarium 4: The Best Canadian Speculative Writing.*

She is an editorial board member at *Canthius* and a creative writing workshop facilitator with the Toronto Writers Collective. Her debut collection of poetry is forthcoming with Mansfield Press in Fall 2017. She lives in Toronto with her husband. To reach out, visit puneetdutt.com, or follow her on Twitter @puneet_dutt.

Susan Ksiezopolski, an award-winning writer has published two poetry anthologies (*My Words* and *Writing for Change*). She has been featured in the Canadian Immigrant magazine, various on-line platforms and has been published in several anthologies (The Ontario Poetry Society *Arborealis* and Mississauga Writers Group "*Canada, our Home*").

Since retiring from public service in 2013, Susan has completed the Humber School for Writers program. She now teaches creative writing workshops across the GTA based on her most recent book "*The Writer's Workbook, Free the Writer Within*". Susan also facilitates workshops for The Toronto Writers Collective and Studio 89 in Mississauga.

Jay Teitel is a Toronto-based writer and editor who has won over 25 National Magazine Awards in categories ranging from Sports to Fiction. He's written two books (*The Argo Bounce* and *From Here to Paternity*) and several screenplays and stage plays, including a musical about his father's journey through Alzheimer's disease (*Alzheimer that ends Heimer*).

He also co-invented the classic board game *Therapy*, which to date has sold more than 3 million copies worldwide. Jay Teitel is currently working on a collection of short stories, and a pilot for a new dramatic television series.

Bänoo Zan is a poet, translator, teacher, editor and poetry curator, with more than 120 published poems and poetry-related pieces as well as three books. *Song of Phoenix: Life and Works of Sylvia Plath*, was reprinted in Iran in 2008. *Songs of Exile*, her first poetry collection, was released in 2016 in Canada by Guernica Editions. *Letters to My Father*, her second poetry book, was released in 2017 by Piquant Press in Canada.

She is the founder of Shab-e She'r (Poetry Night), Toronto's most diverse poetry reading and open mic series. It is a brave space that bridges the gap between communities of poets from different ethnicities, nationalities, religions (or lack thereof), ages, genders, sexual orientations, disabilities, poetic styles, voices and visions.